The Maltese Countryside

Volume 1

A pictorial guide to the Flora of the Maltese Islands

25/05/05.

25/05/05

GUIDO BONETT and JOE ATTARD

The Maltese Countryside

Volume 1

A pictorial guide to the Flora of the Maltese Islands

PUBLICATIONS

Publishers Enterprises Group (PEG) Ltd

Published by
Publishers Enterprises Group (PEG) Ltd,
P.E.G. Building
UB7, Industrial Estate,
San Gwann SGN 09, Malta

E-mail: contact@peg.com.mt
http://www.peg.com.mt

First published 2005

ISBN: 99909-394-8 (paperback)
ISBN: 99909-395-6 (hardback)

Printed by P.E.G. Ltd, Malta

To Jane and Annette

For their patience and support

Acknowledgements

Apart from our personal observations and records, a lot of information presented in this work was gleaned from various sources, both verbal and written, and the authors would like to acknowledge their indebtedness to the many naturalists, past and present, and in particular the authors of the books listed in the references list.

Special thanks are also due to various people who helped in the identification and provided data on some of the species of flora. These include:

Edwin Lanfranco and Sandro Lanfranco.

We are indebted to Michael Calascione and Louis Cassar for their constructive comments and for kindly reading and correcting the manuscript.

We are of course responsible for any errors and imperfections.

We would like to thank James Arrigo, Nicky Attard, Matthew Bonett and Sarah Bonett, for their help, from providing boat transport to the various Islands visited, and help with computer problems. A special thanks goes to Alex Torpiano for making Manoel Island accessible to us.

We would also like to thank Alan Miller and Carmel Psaila (President of the Malta Photographic Society) and Tony Gatt of BDL Ltd whose interest and enthusiasm stimulated us to undertake this project.

Finally we would like to thank Emanuel Debattista, managing director, Gaetan Cilia, Anthony Callus, Kevin Azzopardi and all the staff at P.E.G. Ltd for their continuous support.

Guido Bonett
Joe Attard

Contents

Foreword

One of Din L-Art Ħelwa's primary aims is to promote interest in the preservation and protection of places of beauty and of the natural aspect in Malta, including the animal and plant life of such places.

It is therefore a particular pleasure to introduce a new, excellently illustrated two volume work on the natural history of the Maltese Islands.

Malta is rich in flora and fauna. Despite the relentless tide of construction development of the last half century, there still remain parts of these Islands which are relatively unspoilt. The unique and austere beauty of the natural landscape in Malta is threatened and can only survive if it is protected by those who know it and love it.

This book is designed to fill the need for a well-illustrated, non technical, guide to the flora and fauna of these Islands, to enhance people's knowledge and enjoyment of the countryside and as a result to stimulate interest in the fight for its preservation for future generations to enjoy.

Martin Scicluna
Executive President,
Din l-Art Ħelwa

Author's Preface

We consider ourselves lucky. We have managed to combine our enthusiasm for the natural history of our Islands with our interest in photography, enabling us to enjoy both on a regular basis.

The rich biodiversity of these islands continues to amaze us, and our weekly excursions into valleys, cliff tops and other remote locations has opened a world to us which we suspect is overlooked, or at least not appreciated by the majority of us Maltese and visitors to our archipelago.

The aim of this book is to portray the beauty of Maltese flora and to help the amateur enthusiast, teacher, student and visitor with the identification, from external characteristics, of some of the various species that can be encountered during a country walk.

The flora pictures have mostly been grouped according to colouration for easier identification for those not familiar with scientific plant systematics. In some cases we had the problem of deciding, for example, whether the shade of a flower is more really pink, violet or purple. The text has been kept simple and non technical.

This being a pictorial guide, the species depicted depended on the photo library which we managed to build up during our excursions. It should be noted that all the photographs found in this work where taken in a fourteen month period, from June 2003 to August 2004. Taking these pictures involved numerous visits to Gozo, Comino, Kemmunett and Selmunett, at different times of the year.

The urbanization of our Islands continues apace. Malta and Gozo seem to have become a permanent building site. But there is still a lot of natural beauty and we are still in time to save whatever is left for future generations to enjoy. We would like to think that the pictures in this book will encourage a sense of respect for, and appreciation of the wildlife found on these Islands.

Maquis beneath cliffs – Selmun

Valley – Mġarr ix-Xini, Gozo

Introduction

Malta has many times been called a botanical paradise. This is not surprising, when about 1000 different species have been described and recorded in this archipelago of circa 320 sq. km.

Of the 1000 species, about 800 are indigenous, or native; that is they occur naturally and have not been introduced. The other 200 species are considered to be aliens, introduced by man, either for agricultural or ornamental purposes.

The geographical position of the Maltese Islands results in our flora having similarities with the flora of most of the Mediterranean region, including that of

Clay slopes – Għajn Tuffieħa

Garrigue – Comino

Watercourse – Imselliet

Cliffs – Ta' Ċenċ, Gozo

Sand Dunes – Ir-Ramla l-Ħamra, Gozo

North Africa. The geology of the Islands, and the various environmental factors and habitats thus provided is surely the main reason for such an amazing number of species to occur.

The types of habitat vegetation found on our Islands have all been studied and described in detail in other publications. These biotopes can be short listed into woodland, maquis, garrigue, steppe, clay slopes, valley beds, valley sides, watercourses, saline marshland, cliff tops, cliff faces, and sand dunes. Then of course there is disturbed ground in both urban and rural settings including roadsides, stonewalls and fallow fields.

Malta is host to about twenty endemic species and subspecies of plants, meaning these species are found only in the Maltese Islands. This places the responsibility on us, as Maltese, to safeguard this international heritage. There are also a number of species that are considered rare or endangered locally, sometimes found only in one location either in Malta or Gozo. There are also species that have become extinct in recent years, mainly due to human activities. Unfortunately and undoubtedly there are also species on the way to extinction.

On paper we have a number of laws providing protection to various species, but a short walk in the countryside will soon expose the real situation. Rampant illegal dumping especially common in garrigue and cliff tops, quarries of all types and sizes, buildings and development in ecologically important areas, offroading in certain valleys and on clay slopes and the clearing of garrigue to create bird trapping

Agricultural land – Rabat

Dumping – Chadwick Lakes

Quarries

Rampant buildings – Xemxija

Clearing of Garrigue to make bird trapping sites

Over grazing in certain localities

sites, over-grazing by goats and sheep although on the decline is still a problem in some areas, together with the intentional harvesting of wild flowers for commercial gain are just some of the obvious problems and conditions faced by the local flora (and fauna).

But all is not bleak. Awareness on environmental matters has never been so strong. The environment has become a buzzword even with politicians. The word "Environment" is used hundreds of times everyday in our newspapers. So let us all do our bit to save what is left, through education and persuasion, but also through law enforcement and implementation of sustainable development.

Shades of White

001 FW The bell like flowers of the Bladder Campion

001 FW

English:
Bladder Campion

Maltese:
Qasqejża

Scientific Name:
Silene vulgaris

Flowering period:
March to June

Status:
Frequent

Biotope:
Along rubble walls, country paths and rocky ground

Notes:
Found in most of Europe, North Africa and parts of Temperate Asia

002 FW Flower close-up

002 FW

English:
Chickweed

Maltese:
Ħarira

Soicntific Name:
Stellaria cupaniana

Flowering period:
March to October

Status:
Common

Biotope:
Disturbed ground and gardens

Notes:
Found in most temperate countries

FLORA – SHADES OF WHITE

003 FW Plant profile

003 FW Flower detail

003 FW Seed pod

003 FW

English:
Love-in-a-mist

Maltese:
Sieq il-Brimba

Scientific Name:
Nigella damascena

Flowering period:
March to May

Status:
Common

Biotope:
Disturbed ground, fields

Notes:
A complicated flower, with a bluish tinge, having lace like leaves. Produces large fruits. Frequently cultivated for ornamental purposes

004 FW

English:
Sweet Alison

Maltese:
Buttuniera

Scientific Name:
Lobularia maritima

Flowering period:
All year round

Status:
Very common

Biotope:
Adapted to a variety of different Biotopes, ranging from disturbed ground to garrigue

Notes:
A perennial plant, usually growing prostrate on the ground, rarely more than 50cm high

004 FW Flower close-up

005 FW

English:
Mediterranean Hartwort

Maltese:
Ħaxixet it-Trieraħ

Scientific Name:
Tordylium apulum

Flowering period:
February to April

Status:
Common

Biotope:
Mostly in disturbed ground, but also in garrigue and steppe

Notes:
A plant of the Mediterranean region

005 FW Flower of the Mediterranean Hartwort

006 FW In some localities the flowers can be present in large numbers

006 FW

English:
Sanicle-leaved Water Crowfoot

Maltese:
Ċfolloq ta' l-Ilma

Scientific Name:
Ranunculus saniculaefolius

Flowering period:
January to May

Status:
Frequent but localized

Biotope:
Rainwater pools, especially in garigue

Notes:
This plant produces two kinds of leaves – floating at the surface (broad leaves) and underwater (hairy, finely divided leaves)

006 FW Detail of the Sanicle-leaved Water Crowfoot flower

007 FW

English:
Caper Plant

Maltese:
Kappara

Scientific Name:
Capparis orientalis

Flowering period:
April to September

Status:
Very common

Biotope:
Has adapted to a variety of Biotopes, from mainly cliffs and escarpments, bastion walls, rubble walls and garrigue

Notes:
Local tradition has people pickle the flower buds in vinegar, for use with salads

007 FW Typical flowers and fruit

007 FW Flower detail

007 FW Ripe fruit

008 FW This plant is important as a food plant for various lepidoptera species

008 FW Flower close-up

008 FW

English:
White Mustard

Maltese:
Ġarġir Abjad

Scientific Name:
Diplotaxis erucoides

Flowering period:
All year round

Status:
Very common

Biotope:
Like other very common species, it has adapted to different habitats, but prefers disturbed ground and fields

Notes:
Leaves are edible. It is also a food plant for various species of butterflies, especially of the "Whites"

009 FW

English:
Wild Radish

Maltese:
Ravanell Salvaġġ

Scientific Name:
Raphanus raphanistrum

Flowering period:
December to May

Status:
Common

Biotope:
Mostly found in fields and other disturbed ground

Notes:
Three subspecies are known to occur in Malta. Found throughout Europe

009 FW Sometimes the flowers of the Wild Radish are yellowish

009 FW Some flowers have violet veins

010 FW The Lesser White Clover is an annual species, meaning it completes its whole life cycle in one year

010 FW

English:
Lesser White Clover

Maltese:
Xnien Abjad

Scientific Name:
Trifolium nigrescens

Flowering period:
March to May

Status:
Very common

Biotope:
Garrigue and steppes, but also disturbed ground

Notes:
Found in Southern Europe, North Africa and also western Asia

011 FW

English:
White Mignonette

Maltese:
Denb il-Ħaruf

Scientific Name:
Reseda alba

Flowering period:
December to May

Status:
Common

Biotope:
Disturbed ground, stonewalls and abandoned fields

Notes:
The Maltese name refers to the conical shape that the small flowers form, densely packed, resembling a lamb's tail

011 FW The conical shape that give the species its name

011 FW Flower detail of White Mignonette

012 FW The Bladder Kidney Vetch produces small flowers

012 FW

English:
Bladder Kidney Vetch

Maltese:
Silla tal-Bżieżel

Scientific Name:
Tripodion tetraphyllum

Flowering period:
March to May

Status:
Frequent

Biotope:
Mostly on rocky arid ground and valleys

Notes:
A plant of the Mediterranean region

013 FW Shrub usually carries many flowers

013 FW Flower close-up

013 FW Unique patch of Narrow-leaved Rock-rose habitat destroyed

013 FW

English:
Narrow-leaved Rock-rose

Maltese:
Ċistu Abjad

Scientific Name:
Cistus monspeliensis

Flowering period:
March to May

Status:
Rare. Found only in one locality in Malta, and one other locality in Gozo

Biotope:
Garrigue

Notes:
Considering the vulnerability of this species, one is baffled to see that people are actually allowed to clear large tracts of habitat, in the only site in Malta where the species is found, plants and all, in order to setup bird trapping sites. Surely this species deserves better protection

014 FW In places the species is very common

014 FW The umbellate of the Wild Carrot in fruit

014 FW The umbellate host the Striped Shield Bug, sometimes in large numbers, where they mate and probably lay their ova

014 FW Flowers can be white, pink or purple

014 FW

English:
Wild Carrot

Maltese:
Żunnarija Salvaġġa

Scientific Name:
Daucus carota

Flowering period:
April to July

Status:
Very common

Biotope:
Grows practically everywhere, in all types of habitats

Notes:
Possibly several subspecies are to be found in Malta, but still give the experts headaches. The flowers can be white or pinkish. They attract many species of insects, especially in the summer months, when other flowers are scarce

FLORA – SHADES OF WHITE

015 FW

English:
Olive-leaved Bindweed

Maltese:
Leblieb tal-Blat

Scientific Name:
Convolvulus oleifolius

Flowering period:
March to October

Status:
Frequent

Biotope:
Garrigue, usually not far from the sea-shore, and along cliff tops

Notes:
The flowers can be white or pink, usually forming a dense shrub sometimes with hundreds of flowers

015 FW The Olive-leaved Bindweed flower is variable, from white to pink

016 FW

English:
Yellow Germander

Maltese:
Borgħom Komuni

Scientific Name:
Teucrium flavum

Flowering period:
April to July

Status:
Common

Biotope:
Garrigue, maquis and valley sides

Notes:
A hairy shrub with flowering stems up to 50cm. high, each stem carrying a number of flowers

016 FW Flowers are borne on 50 cm stems

016 FW Flower close-up

017 FW Typical flowers

017 FW Bracts are sometimes violet, not the usual green

017 FW

English:
Honeywort

Maltese:
Qniepen

Scientific Name:
Cerinthe major

Flowering period:
January to May

Status:
Common

Biotope:
Disturbed ground, but also damp valleys and maquis

Notes:
A plant of the Mediterranean region. One of the earliest spring flowers to appear

017 FW Early leaves are usually spotted

018 FW

English:
Common Heliotrope

Maltese:
Vanilja Bajda

Scientific Name:
Heliotropium europapaeum

Flowering period:
April to October

Status:
Very common

Biotope:
Disturbed ground, fields and gardens

Notes:
Small flowers carried on curved inflorescence

018 FW The leaves are greyish

018 FW The flowers are small

019 FW Sometimes forms dense shrubs

019 FW Flower close-up shows a purplish tinge

019 FW

English:
White Hedge-nettle

Maltese:
Te Sqalli

Scientific Name:
Prasium majus

Flowering period:
January to June

Status:
Common

Biotope:
Mostly garrigue and maquis

Notes:
In some localities it is the dominant species, forming dense shrubs on walls and in between boulders

020 FW Black berries of the Black Nightshade

020 FW

English:
Black Nightshade

Maltese:
Gheneb id-Dib

Scientific Name:
Solanum nigrum

Flowering period:
All year round

Status:
Common

Biotope:
Like the Hairy Nightshade, in waste ground and in the shade of trees

Notes:
Produces poisonous, dark green or black berries

021 FW

English:
Hairy Nightshade

Maltese:
Tuffieħ is-Serp

Scientific Name:
Solanum villosum

Flowering period:
April to November

Status:
Common

Biotope:
Under trees and disturbed ground

Notes:
Produces poisonous, red, orange or yellowish berries

021 FW Flower close-up

021 FW The poisonous red berries

022 FW Sicilian Snapdragon

022 FW

English:
Sicilian Snapdragon

Maltese:
Papoċċi Bajda

Scientific Name:
Antirrhinum siculum

Flowering period:
All year round

Status:
Common

Biotope:
Walls, fortifications, disturbed ground

Notes:
From Sicily has spread across Southern Europe

023 FW

English:
Bear's Breeches

Maltese:
Ħannewija

Scientific Name:
Acanthus mollis

Flowering period:
March to June

Status:
Common

Biotope:
Maquis, disturbed ground and sheltered woody areas

Notes:
Large leaves and 1m high, erect inflorescence make this plant impressive when found in large numbers

023 FW Undeveloped inflorescence

023 FW Inflorescence in its prime

023 FW Flower detail

023 FW Seeds

023 FW Leaves of Bear's Breeches

024 FW

English:
Greater Thorn-apple

Maltese:
Siġret ir-Rizzi

Scientific Name:
Datura innoxia

Flowering period:
May to December

Status:
Not common

Biotope:
Public gardens, ditches

Notes:
Originally from Central America, has become naturalized in most of the Mediterranean region. Fruits are covered in spines, hence the Maltese name "Sea Urchin Plant". Flowers, leaves and fruit are all very poisonous

024 FW The flowers can be up to 20 cm long

025 FW

English:
Dwarf Broomrape

Maltese:
Budebbus ta' l-ingliża

Scientific Name:
Orobanche muteli

Flowering period:
March to May

Status:
Common

Biotope:
Mostly valleys, but also garrigue and maquis

Notes:
A parasite of the Cape Sorrel. The smallest broomrape on the islands, of which there are several species

025 FW Flower close-up

025 FW A common sight in our countryside – The dwarf Broomrape

026 FW

English:
Southern Daisy

Maltese:
Margerita Salvaġġa

Scientific Name:
Bellis sylvestris

Flowering period:
September to March

Status:
Common

Biotope:
Valleys

Notes:
Flowers are carried on stalks that can be 30cms high, and close at dusk

026 FW The numerous petals are narrow and long when compared to other Daisy species

027 FW Flower close-up

027 FW

English:
Maltese Sea Chamomile

Maltese:
Bebuna tal-Baħar

Scientific Name:
Anthemis urvilleana

Flowering period:
March to June

Status:
Common

Biotope:
Always near the coast

Notes:
An endemic species, in places forming large mats of flowers

027 FW Forms large mats of flowers where the conditions are right

028 FW The Branched Asphodel – a familiar sight in early spring

028 FW Flower close-up

028 FW

English:
Branched Asphodel

Maltese:
Berwieq

Scientific Name:
Asphodelus aestivus

Flowering period:
December to May

Status:
Very Common

Biotope:
Steppe and arid rocky places

Notes:
Robust stems can be up to 150 cms high, carrying large numbers of flowers. The Branched Asphodel is host ta a Longhorn Beetle *Agapanthia asphodeli* which is only ever found perched on the stem of the plant in late March and early April

028 FW The stems carry a large number of flowers

028 FW The Longhorn beetle *Agapanthia asphodeli*

029 FW Flower head of the Hairy Garlic

029 FW The branched stalks can be up to 30 cm high

029 FW

English:
Hairy Garlic

Maltese:
Tewm Muswaf

Scientific Name:
Allium subhirsutum

Flowering period:
March to May

Status:
Very common

Biotope:
Garrigue and valleys in rocky areas

Notes:
A member of the Lily family, these plants are in many ways similar to the cultivated garlic. Each plant can have a number of flowers on a branched stalk that is about 30 cm high

030 FW The plant does not have much in common with that of the related Branched Asphodel

030 FW The striped buds of the Pink Asphodel

030 FW Flower detail

030 FW The flowers of the Pink Asphodel are smaller than those of the Branched Asphodel

030 FW

English:
Pink Asphodel

Maltese:
Berwieq Żgħir

Scientific Name:
Asphodelus fistulosus

Flowering period:
February to May

Status:
Rare

Biotope:
Rocky areas and fortifications

Notes:
Plant never more than 50 cm high. Flowers much smaller than that of A. aestivus, and more pinkish

031 FW Flower detail

031 FW Numerous flowers are to be found on each plant

031 FW

English:
Southern Star of Bethlehem

Maltese:
Ħalib it-Tajr Żgħir

Scientific Name:
Ornithogalum narbonense

Flowering period:
March to May

Status:
Frequent

Biotope:
Areas with small stones and rocks, especially around fields

Notes:
A species of the Mediterranean region, extending into Asia

032 FW

English:
Large Star of Bethlehem

Maltese:
Ħalib it-Tajr Kbir

Scientific Name:
Ornithogalum arabicum

Flowering period:
April to May

Status:
Frequent

Biotope:
Garrigue, Steppe and disused fields

Notes:
Unfortunately seems to be on the decline

032 FW The collection of this flower for commercial purposes is taking its toll on the species

032 FW Close-up of the Large Star of Betlehem

033 FW September – flowers of Sea Squill

033 FW

English:
Sea Squill

Maltese:
Għansar

Scientific Name:
Urginea maritima

Flowering period:
August and September

Status:
Very Common

Biotope:
Arid and rocky places

Notes:
An impressive species, with a bulb that is 15 cm in diameter, and a large number of flowers on a 100 cm stem, all disappearing in autumn when the big leaves start to emerge. The bulb seems to be a favoured food item for wild rabbits as one often comes across bulbs that have been exposed and nibbled

033 FW August – developing stem of Sea Squill

033 FW August – Sea Squill flower buds

033 FW October – Sea Squill bulbs sprouting

033 FW November – leaves of Sea Squill

033 FW September – 100 cm high flowering stem of Sea Squill

034 FW Stalk with developing flowers

034 FW Each umbel could carry from 3 to 12 flowers

034 FW The spirally twisted leaves

034 FW Close-up of the heavily scented flower

034 FW

English:
Sea Daffodil

Maltese:
Pankrazju

Scientific Name:
Pancratium maritimum

Flowering period:
June to October

Status:
Scarce and localised due to rarity of habitat

Biotope:
Sandy beaches and dunes

Notes:
The future of the species is bleak, unless the few remaining dunal assemblages are properly protected

034 FW The fruit capsule

034 FW In certain localities some of the flowers are inhabited by juvenile bush-crickets *Platycleis tessellata*

035 FW

English:
Autumn Narcissus

Maltese:
Narċis Imwaħħar

Scientific Name:
Narcissus serotinus

Flowering period:
September to November

Status:
Frequent

Biotope:
Garrigue and rocky arid places

Notes:
This flower can found just after the first rains, usually in September. It does not form bunches like the other Narcissus species

035 FW This flower is commonly found after the first rains

036 FW Flowerhead

036 FW

English:
Round-headed Water-dropwort

Maltese:
—

Scientific Name:
Oenanthe globulosa

Flowering period:
March to May

Status:
Frequent

Biotope:
Watercourses

Notes:
Branched stems up to 50 cm high. A species of the Mediterranean region, including North Africa

036 FW Fruit

037 FW In the wild, French Daffodils can be a spectacular sight when present in large numbers

037 FW These flowers are picked and sold in large numbers because of their strong scent

037 FW Flower close-ups

037 FW

English:
French Daffodil

Maltese:
Narċis

Scientific Name:
Narcissus tazetta

Flowering period:
October to March

Status:
Frequent

Biotope:
Field verges, valleys and steppes

Notes:
Unfortunately still collected for sale in large numbers

038 FW

English:
Annual Daisy

Maltese:
Bebuna

Scientific Name:
Bellis annua

Flowering period:
December to April

Status:
Common

Biotope:
Rocky places and valleys

Notes:
When growing in favorable conditions forms a densely flowered bush

038 FW In favorable conditions this plant forms multi-flowered bushes

039 FW Flower detail of Iris

039 FW Typical flower

039 FW

English:
Iris

Maltese:
Fjurdulis Abjad

Scientific Name:
Iris florentina

Flowering period:
February to May

Status:
Rare

Biotope:
Garrigue and rocky steppe

Notes: Plant 30 to 80 cm high. The local name is derived from the French Fleur-de-Lys

040 FW Leaves of the Italian Lords-and-Ladies

040 FW Forming fruit

040 FW Ripe fruit

040 FW Bract

040 FW

English:
Italian Lords-and-Ladies

Maltese:
Garni

Scientific Name:
Arum italicum

Flowering period:
March to May

Status:
Common

Biotope:
Disturbed ground, maquis, under trees and valley-beds

Notes:
The minute flowers are yellow, densely formed to form a finger like stalk, all wrapped in a large greenish papery bract

041 FW

English:
Common Smilax

Maltese:
Pajżana

Scientific Name:
Smilax aspera

Flowering period:
September to November

Status:
Frequent

Biotope:
Maquis and valleys in rocky sheltered places

Notes:
A woody climber, which can be very thorny, but not always. Also, the shape and colour of the leaves varies. The white flowers are followed by bunches of red berries

041 FW Leaf with some thorns on edges

041 FW Berries of the Common Smilax

042 FW Mediterranean Starfruit growing in a rock pool

042 FW

English:
Mediterranean Starfruit

Maltese:
Damażonju

Scientific Name:
Damasonium bourgaei

Flowering period:
March to May

Status:
Rare

Biotope:
In freshwater rock pools in garrigue

Notes:
Small flowers white, with three petals. The species is rare because of it's specialised habitat requirements. The leaves change from a flat papery kind when water is available, becoming more robust and erect when the water dries up

043 FW

English:
Spiny Echinophore

Maltese:
Busbies Xewwieki tar-Ramel

Scientific Name:
Echinophora spinosa

Flowering period:
April to September

Status:
Rare and endangered

Biotope:
Sand dunes

Notes:
Spiny shrub reaching height of 50 cm. White flowers held in umbrella-shaped inflorescences. Vulnerable because the species is to be found only in sand dunes. A Mediterranean species

043 FW Inflorescence of white flowers

043 FW Close-up of the spiny rigid stems

044 FW This flower superficially resembles the Crown Daisy, but is all white

044 FW

English:
White Anacyclus

Maltese:
—

Scientific Name:
Anacyclus clavatus

Flowering period:
June to July

Status:
Rare

Biotope:
Steppes and clayey soil

Notes:
Low growing shrub. A species of the Mediterranean region

045 FW

English:
Willow-leaved Knotgrass

Maltese:
Persikarja

Scientific Name:
Persicaria senegalensis

Flowering period:
May to September

Status:
Rare

Biotope:
Damp places and watercourses

Notes:
Stout stems up to 70 cm high

045 FW The inflorescence of the Willow-leaved Knotgrass

045 FW In this case the plant is growing close to the ground, showing the lance like leaves

046 FW The stem and leaves are hairy

046 FW

English:
Black Horebound

Maltese:
Marrubja sewda

Scientific Name:
Ballota nigra

Flowering period:
April to November

Status:
Frequent

Biotope:
Damp valleys, wooded areas

Notes:
Hairy stems up to 120 cm. Found in most of Europe and the Mediterranean region

047 FW

English:
Common Sideritis

Maltese:
—

Scientific Name:
Siderites romana

Flowering period:
March to June

Status:
Frequent

Biotope:
Carrigue and also fallow fields

Notes:
Never more than 30 cm high. A species of the Mediterranean region

047 FW The small flowers have a hint of pink

Shades of Yellow

001 FY The leaves are deeply lobed

001 FY

English:
Perennial Hyoseris

Maltese:
Żigland tal-Pizzi

Scientific Name:
Hyoseris radiata

Flowering period:
December to April

Status:
Common

Biotope:
Damp Valleys

Notes:
A species of the Mediterranean region

002 FY Flower close-up

002 FY

English:
Autumn Buttercup

Maltese:
Ċfolloq

Scientific Name:
Ranunculus bullatus

Flowering period:
October to February

Status:
Common

Biotope:
Maquis, garrigue and steppe

Notes:
Mediterranean region, including North Africa

003 FY Showing elongated fruit

003 FY Hairy buds

003 FY Leaves

003 FY Flower close-up

003 FY

English: Yellow Horned-poppy

Maltese:
Pepprin Isfar

Scientific Name:
Glaucium flavum

Flowering period:
April to July

Status:
Common

Biotope:
Coastal, especially in sandy areas

Notes:
Leaves bluish grey, hairy, and bears elongated fruit

004 FY

English:
Scilly Buttercup

Maltese:
Ċfolloq

Scientific Name:
Ranunculus muricatus

Flowering period:
February to May

Status:
Common

Biotope:
Humid valleys

Notes:
A widespread species, originating in the Mediterranean and extending as far as India

004 FY The leaves are deeply cut

005 FY Showing hairy stem and leaves of Bargeman's Cabbage

005 FY Flower close-up

005 FY

English:
Bargeman's Cabbage

Maltese:
Liftija

Scientific Name:
Brassica rapa ssp.silvestris

Flowering period:
November to May

Status:
Very common

Biotope:
Disturbed ground and cultivated fields

Notes:
Stems can be 150 cm high. Widespread in Europe and the Mediterranean region

006 FY Leaves of the Mediterranean Stonecrop

006 FY Flowers on stalk

006 FY

English:
Mediterranean Stonecrop

Maltese:
Sedum

Scientific Name:
Sedum sediforme

Flowering period:
June to July

Status:
Common

Biotope:
Coastal garrigue and cliff tops

Notes:
Flowering stems can be up to 60 cm high, and flowers can be either white or pale yellow

007 FY

English:
Creeping Cinquefoil

Maltese:
Frawla Salvaġġa

Scientific Name:
Potentilla reptans

Flowering period:
March to June

Status:
Frequent but localised

Biotopc:
Valley bottoms especially along stream beds

Notes:
Flowering stems up to 100 cm high

007 FY Flower detail

007 FY Leaves

008 FY The flowers are small, and the leaves trifoliate

008 FY
English:
Mediterranean Melilot

Maltese:
Trew Komuni

Scientific Name:
Melilotus sulcatus

Flowering period:
January to May

Status:
Very Common

Biotope:
Fields, disturbed ground

Notes:
A Mediterranean species, usually not more than 40 cm high

009 FY

English:
Bushy Restharrow

Maltese:
Broxka ta' Għawdex

Scientific Name:
Ononis natrix ssp.ramosissima

Flowering period:
April to May

Status:
Localised

Biotope:
Coastal garrigue and cliff tops

Notes:
More common in Gozo than in Malta. Forms a dense shrub up to 80 cm high. Used to be collected for firewood

009 FY Flower close-up

009 FY Flowers of the Bushy Restharrow entwined in spider's web with dew drops

010 FY Flower detail

010 FY

English:
Sea Medick

Maltese:
Nefel tar-Ramel

Scientific Name:
Medicago marina

Flowering period:
March to May

Status:
Very rare

Biotope:
Sand dunes

Notes:
Unfortunately has become very rare, probably found only in one location and needs urgent protection

010 FY Sea Medick

010 FY Typical habitat of the Sea Medick

010 FY Sea Medick – leaf detail

011 FY

English:
Hop Trefoil

Maltese:
Xnien Isfar

Scientific Name:
Trifolium campestre

Flowering period:
March to May

Status:
Common

Biotope:
Garrigue and steppe

Notes:
Low lying plant, usually not more than 30 cm high

The leaves are trifoliate, and the flowers small

011 FY The leaves are trifoliate, and the flowers small

012 FY

English:
Common Birdsfoot Trefoil

Maltese:
Qrempuċ tal-Mogħoż

Scientific Name:
Lotus ornithopodioides

Flowering period:
February to May

Status:
Very common

Biotope:
Grows in most habitat-types

Notes:
Up to 50 cm high. Flowers usually in clusters of 3 to 5

012 FY A cluster of four flowers

013 FY Flower close-up

013 FY

English:
Grey Birdsfoot Trefoil

Maltese:
Ghantux tal-Blat

Scientific Name:
Lotus cytisoides

Flowering period:
February to June

Status:
Frequent

Biotope:
Garrigue and rocky coasts

Notes:
Forms a small shrub up to 50 cm high. A plant found only in the Mediterranean region

013 FY This plant forms a small shrub

014 FY

English:
Shrubby Kidney Vetch

Maltese:
Ħatba Sewda

Scientific Name:
Anthyllis hermanniae

Flowering period:
March to June

Status:
frequent

Biotope:
Garrigue (more specifically Phrygana)

Notes:
Forms dense shrub up to 60 cm high, sometimes completely covered by the small yellow flowers

014 FY Flower detail

014 FY Shrub in typical habitat

015 FY The leaves of the Upright Yellow Flax are narrow

015 FY Flower close-up

015 FY

English:
Upright Yellow Flax

Maltese:
Kittien Isfar

Scientific Name:
Linum strictum

Flowering period:
March to May

Status:
Common

Biotope:
Garrigue, steppe and disturbed ground

Notes:
Erect stems usually not more than 40 cm high

016 FY

English:
Common Horseshoe Vetch

Maltese:
Xintilli Komuni

Scientific Name:
Hippocrepis multisiliquosa

Flowering period:
March to May

Status:
Common

Biotope:
Garrigue, steppes and disturbed ground

Notes:
Up to 60 cm high. A species of the Mediterranean region

016 FY Showing the pinnate leaves, stem growing low

016 FY The flowerhead

017 FY Flower close-up

017 FY

English:
Scorpion-tail Vetch

Maltese:
Widna

Scientific Name:
Scorpiurus muricatus

Flowering period:
March to May

Status:
Common

Biotope:
Valleys, garrigue and steppes

Notes:
Cultivated as a forage plant

018 FY Flowers of the Thyme-leaved Sun-Rose are smaller than those of the Mediterranean Sun-Rose

018 FY

English:
Thyme-leaved Sun-rose

Maltese:
Ċistu Żgħir

Scientific Name:
Fumana thymifolia

Flowering period:
March to May

Status:
Frequent

Biotope:
Garrigue

Notes:
Usually found growing with the Mediterranean Sun-rose. The flowers are much smaller, with the plant not more than 20 cm high

019 FY A Cape Sorrel plant produces many flowers

019 FY Flower detail

019 FY Double-Flowered Cape Sorrel

019 FY

English:
Cape Sorrel

Maltese:
Ħaxixa Ingliża

Scientific Name:
Oxalis pes-caprae

Flowering period:
November to May

Status:
Very common

Biotope:
Ubiquitous to most habitats

Notes:
Introduced in 1811 to the botanical gardens in Floriana, from where it escaped and thereafter spread throughout the Mediterranean.
There is a double flowered form which is not as common

019 FY Leaves of Cape Sorrel

020 FY The whole plant

020 FY Leaves of the Fringed Rue, which when crushed are very aromatic

020 FY Flower close-up

020 FY

English:
Fringed Rue

Maltese:
Fejġel

Scientific Name:
Ruta chalepensis

Flowering period:
March to June

Status:
Frequent

Biotope:
Garrigue and rocky steppe

Notes:
Aromatic plant up to 60 cm high. Mediterranean region and Atlantic Islands. The Fringed Rue is one of the larval food plants of the Swallowtail Butterfly

021 FY The Egyptian St.John's-wort forms a dense shrub

021 FY The leaves are small and fleshy

021 FY Flower close-up

021 FY

English:
Egyptian St.John's-wort

Maltese:
Fexfiex ta' l-Irdum

Scientific Name:
Hypericum aegyptiacum

Flowering period:
January to June

Status:Frequent

Biotope:
Coastal and cliff top garrigue (more specifically Phrygana)

Notes:
Forms a dense shrub. A species of the Mediterranean region

022 FY

English:
Crisped St.John's-wort

Maltese:
Fexfiex tar-Raba'

Scientific Name:
Hypericum triquetrifolium

Flowering period:
March to October

Status:
Common

Biotope:
Cultivated and disturbed ground

Notes:
Flowers most prominent in summer. Stems can be 50 cm high. Found in the Mediterranean region into Western Asia

022 FY Flower detail

022 FY The small leaves

023 FY Many flowers are produced by each plant

023 FY

English:
Mediterranean Sun-rose

Maltese:
Ċistu Isfar

Scientific Name:
Fumana arabica

Flowering period:
March to May

Status:
Common

Biotope:
Arid rocky terrain, garrigue

Notes:
Plant can be up to 35 cm high, with many flowers. A plant of the Mediterranean region

023 FY Flower close-up

024 FY

English:
Pubescent St.John's-wort

Maltese:
Fexfiex Sufi

Scientific Name:
Hypericum pubescens

Flowering period:
April to July

Status:
Common

Biotope:
Garrigue, steppe and sometimes disturbed rocky ground

Notes:
The name refers to the hairy nature of the plant. Stems can be up to 90 cm. Not very widespread, found mainly in Portugal, Spain and Sicily besides Malta

024 FY Flower close-up

024 FY Creeping plant, a characteristic of the species

025 FY The yellow-wort grows to a height of 50 cm

025 FY Flower close-up

025 FY

English:
Yellow-wort

Maltese:
Ċentawrja Safra

Scientific Name:
Blackstonia perfoliata

Flowering period:
March to May

Status:
Frequent

Biotope:
Garrigue and rocky steppe

Notes:
An erect plant, usually from 10 to 50 cm high. Grows in the same areas as the Common Centaury, but is never as plentiful

026 FY Leaf structure

026 FY Flower of the Squirting Cucumber

026 FY Fruit

026 FY

English:
Squirting Cucumber

Maltese:
Faqqus il-Ħmir

Scientific Name:
Ecballium elaterium

Flowering period:
Throughout the year

Status:
Very common

Biotope:
Disturbed ground

Notes:
Fruit about 4 cm, oval and covered in hairs. Plant usually up to 60 cm high. Mediterranean region

026 FY The Gourd Ladybird feeds and lives on the Squirting Cucumber exclusively

027 FY Sweet scented leaves

027 FY Umbels developing

027 FY

English:
Fennel

Maltese:
Bużbież

Scientific Name:
Foeniculum vulgare

Flowering period:
May to October

Status:
Very common

Biotope:
Recently abandoned fields, road verges and degraded areas

Notes:
Sweet scented leaves filiform, with stems up to 200 cm high, sometimes more. It is one of the two food plants for the larvae of the Swallowtail Butterfly. Found in most of Europe and North Africa

027 FY Yellow-flowered umbels

028 FY

English:
Alexanders

Maltese:
Karfus il-Ħmir

Scientific Name:
Smyrnium olusatrum

Flowering period:
February to April

Status:
Very Common

Biotope:
Shaded areas in valleys, under trees and also disturbed terrain

Notes:
Up to 120 cm high, with large Celery like leaves, hence the Maltese name

028 FY The leaves resemble those of Celery, hence the Maltese name

028 FY Umbel with flowers

029 FY The leaves arranged in whorls

029 FY

English:
Wild Madder

Maltese:
Robbja Salvaġġa

Scientific Name:
Rubia peregrina

Flowering period:
April to June

Status:
Common

Biotope:
Maquis, Woodland

Notes:
A climber, with stems reaching 120 cm. Small flowers present in large numbers. Mediterranean region and western Europe

029 FY The very small flowers growing on multi branched Inflorescences

030 FY Leaves

030 FY Unfurling umbels

030 FY Plant profile

030 FY

English:
Giant Fennel

Maltese:
Ferla

Scientific Name:
Ferula communis

Flowering period:
March to May

Status:
Very common

Biotope:
Abandoned fields, degraded areas, steppe garrigue and maquis

Notes:
Robust stem up to 200 cm high. A species that is characteristic of our countryside

030 FY Giant Fennel flowerheads attract many species of insects

030 FY Fully developed umbels of the Giant Fennel

030 FY Seeds

FLORA – SHADES OF YELLOW

031 FY

English:
Coast Ragwort

Maltese:
Kromb tax-Xatt

Scientific Name:
Senecio leucanthemifolius

Flowering period:
February to April

Status:
Relatively rare

Biotope:
Coastal rocky areas

Notes:
Plant up to 40 cm high, with fleshy leaves. Found in the western and Central Mediterranean

031 FY Usually found growing close to the sea

032 FY Bush and flower density of the Great Sage can be substantial in some localities

032 FY Flower close-up

032 FY

English:
Great sage

Maltese:
Salvja tal-Madonna

Scientific Name:
Phlomis fruticosa

Flowering period:
March to June

Status:
Frequent

Biotope:
Karstic terrain, usually within garrigue and rocky valley sides

Notes:
Shrub up to 130 cm high, with large velvety yellow flowers, and with grayish leaves covered in hair. A species of Southern Europe

032 FY Great Sage flowers are velvety

033 FY Showing the hairy leaves

033 FY Fruit

033 FY Flower close-up

033 FY

English:
White Henbane

Maltese:
Mammażejża

Scientific Name:
Hyoscyamus albus

Flowering period:
All year round

Status:
Common

Biotope:
Disturbed ground, walls and rubble

Notes:
Stems from 30 to 90 cm, woody at the base. Mediterranean region

034 FY

English:
Shrub Tobacco

Maltese:
Tabakk tas-Swar

Scientific Name:
Nicotiana glauca

Flowering period:
April to October

Status:
Common

Biotope:
Disturbed ground including sites with building debris

Notes:
Up to 400 cm high. A native of South America, has become naturalized in most of the Mediterranean region

034 FY The leaves are large and smooth

034 FY Flowers grow in bunches

035 FY Small shrub growing on rock

035 FY

English:
Maltese Fleabane

Maltese:
Tulliera ta' Malta

Scientific Name:
Chiliadenus bocconei

Flowering period:
May to October

Status:
Common

Biotope:
Garrigue and rocky steppe

Notes:
An endemic species. Forms a small shrub, with a strong smell of camphor when the leaves are crushed

035 FY Flower detail

036 FY

English:
Wavy-leaved Mullein

Maltese:
Xatbet l-Andar

Scientific Name:
Verbascum sinuatum

Flowering period:
May to August

Status:
Common

Biotope:
Disturbed ground, particularly roadsides

Notes:
Rigid stem up to 100 cm high, freely branched with many flowers. Found in most of Europe, North Africa and into Western Asia

036 FY Flower close-up

036 FY Flower detail

036 FY Branched main stem can carry many flowers

037 FY Habitat

037 FY

English:
Sticky Fleabane

Maltese:
Tulliera Komuni

Scientific Name:
Dittrichia viscosa

Flowering period:
July to November

Status:
Very common

Biotope:
Most habitat-types

Notes:
Forms shrub up to 130 cm high, woody at the base. Sticky leaves aromatic

037 FY Leaf detail of the Sticky Fleabane

037 FY Flower close-up

038 FY Close-up of the very small flower

038 FY

English:
Southern Flax

Maltese:
–

Scientific Name:
Linum trigynum

Flowering period:
March to May

Status:
Frequent

Biotope:
Garrigue

Notes:
Very small flower, with petals 4-6 mm. Stem up to 30 cm

039 FY Plant profile

039 FY Leaves

039 FY Flower detail

039 FY

English:
Maltese Everlasting

Maltese:
Sempreviva ta' Għawdex

Scientific Name:
Helichrysum melitense

Flowering period:
March to June

Status:
Rare

Biotope:
Cliffs

Notes:
An endemic species, found only in one locality in Gozo, probably extinct in Malta. Forms bush about 100 cm high. Leaves whitish covered with hair. Protected by law, but left to the mercy of the public

039 FY Typical habitat of the Maltese Everlasting

040 FY **Detail of flower**

040 FY

English:
Hairy Broomrape

Maltese:
Budebbus tal-Lellux

Scientific Name:
Orobanche pubescens

Flowering period:
March to May

Status:
Frequent

Biotope:
Disturbed ground and abandoned fields

Notes:
Can reach 50 cm high. Parasitic on the Crown Daisy

040 FY Usually found growing with the Crown Daisy and Alexanders

041 FY This flowering plant is similar but not as common as the Bellardia

041 FY

English:
Yellow Eye-bright

Maltese:
Perlina Safra

Scientific Name:
Parentucellia viscosa

Flowering period:
March to May

Status:
Frequent

Biotope:
Garrigue and steppe

Notes:
Usually found growing with the similar Bellardia

042 FY Flowers forming small shrub

042 FY Dried flower-heads

042 FY Flower detail

042 FY

English:
Eastern Phagnalon

Maltese:
Lixka Komuni

Scientific Name:
Phagnalon graecum ssp. ginzbergeri

Flowering period:
March to May

Status:
Common

Biotope:
Garrigue and rocky steppe

Notes:
A small shrub, usually not more than 30 cm high. Native to South Eastern Europe

043 FY

English:
Golden Samphire

Maltese:
Xorbett

Scientific Name:
Inula crithmoides

Flowering period:
June to November

Status:
Common

Biotope:
Coastal areas

Notes:
Shrub, up to 100 cm high. Leaves fleshy. Found along all the coasts of the Mediterranean region

043 FY Fleshy leaves

043 FY Flower close-up

043 FY Flower detail

044 FY In places can form extensive mats

044 FY

English:
Seaside Ox-eye Daisy

Maltese:
Għajn il-Baqra tax-Xatt

Scientific Name:
Nauplius aquaticus

Flowering period:
April to June

Status:
Frequent

Biotope:
Coastal, in both rocky and sandy areas

Notes:
Rigid branched stems up to 50 cm high. More common on the smaller islands, sometimes present in large numbers

044 FY Flower close-up

045 FY

English:
Spiny Ox-eye Daisy

Maltese:
Għajn il-Baqra
Xewwikija

Scientific Name:
Pallenis spinosa

Flowering period:
April to June

Status:
Common

Biotope:
Mostly coastal garrigue, steppes and disturbed ground

Notes:
Hard branched stems up to 50 cm high. Mediterranean region

045 FY Flower detail

045 FY Typical plant

046 FY Crown Daisy close-up

046 FY

English:
Crown Daisy

Maltese:
Lellux

Scientific Name:
Chrysanthemum coronarium

Flowering period:
January to June

Status:
Very common

Biotope:
Disturbed ground

Notes:
Stems up to 60 cm high. Mediterranean region

046 FY Normal variety of the Crown Daisy

046 FY The variety *discolor*

047 FY This species has adapted to a variety of habitats. It is here growing in sand dunes

047 FY

English:
Smooth Sow-thistle

Maltese:
Tfief

Scientific Name:
Sonchus oleraceus

Flowering period:
January to May

Status:
Very common

Biotope:
Grows everywhere

Notes:
Stems up to 150 cm high, usually branched. Various other similar species are to be found

047 FY This flower is very familiar. It is harvested mostly to be fed to rabbits

048 FY Plant showing leaves

048 FY

English:
Gozo Hyoseris

Maltese:
Żigland ta' Għawdex

Scientific Name:
Hyoseris frutescens

Flowering period:
All year round

Status:
Rare

Biotope:
Coastal cliffs, in humid cracks in rocky areas

Notes:
An endemic species, more common in Gozo than in Malta. The lobed leaves are fleshy

048 FY Flower close-up

049 FY Leaves

049 FY The flowers are host to a variety of beetle species

049 FY Plant profile

049 FY

English:
Silvery Ragwort

Maltese:
Kromb il-Baħar Isfar

Scientific Name:
Senecio bicolor

Flowering period:
May to July

Status:
Common

Biotope:
Mostly coastal rocky terrain, but also inland in valleys

Notes:
Shrub up to 100 cm high. Fleshy leaves mostly at the base of the branched stems, green above and silvery below. Sometimes red leaves present

050 FY

English:
Great Lettuce

Maltese:
Ħass Xewwieki

Scientific Name:
Lactuca virosa

Flowering period:
May to August

Status:
Common

Biotope:
Urban waste ground and roadsides

Notes:
Can be 200 cm high, with large prickly leaves

050 FY Leaves

050 FY Spines on leaf

050 FY Flowers

051 FY Small flowers

051 FY

English:
Spiny Asparagus

Maltese:
Spraġ Xewwieki

Scientific Name:
Asparagus aphyllus

Flowering period:
Flowers twice:
August to December
and March to May

Status:
Common

Biotope:
Woodland, maquis
and garrigue

Notes:
Shrub with stems up to 150 cm. Sometimes clambers over other vegetation. Very spiny

051 FY Fruit

052 FY New leaves

052 FY Typical plant

052 FY Flower detail

052 FY

English:
Bristly Oxtongue

Maltese:
–

Scientific Name:
Picris echioides

Flowering period:
March to August

Status:
Frequent

Biotope:
Disturbed ground and clayey soil

Notes:
Stems up to 100 cm high, leaves hairy, sometimes with spines. A widespread species from Southern Europe into South West Asia

053 FY

English:
Southern Bugle

Maltese:
Xantkura

Scientific Name:
Ajuga iva

Flowering period:
January to June

Status:
Frequent

Biotope:
Garrigue and disturbed ground

Notes:
The flowers are more commonly pinkish (refer to shades of red and pink, p.157)

053 FY The elongated leaves are hairy

053 FY These uncommon yellow flowers have red dots placed in 2 rows

054 FY The leaves are spear shaped

054 FY

English:
Spear-leaved Hare's-ear

Maltese:
Widnet il-Fenek

Scientific Name:
Bupleurum lancifolium

Flowering period:
March to May

Status:
Localised

Biotope:
Valleys and cultivated areas

Notes:
Mediterranean region north to Central Europe and Asia Minor

054 FY Flower detail

055 FY

English:
Prickly Golden-fleece

Maltese:
Tfief Xewwieki

Scientific Name:
Urospermum picroides

Flowering period:
January to June

Status:
Common

Biotope:
Steppes and fields

Notes:
Stems up to 45 cm high with rigid hairs and spines

055 FY The stems are covered with rigid hairs

055 FY Flower close-up

Shades of Red and Pink

001 FRP The narrow and long leaves are hairy

001 FRP

English:
Southern Bugle

Maltese:
Xantkura

Scientific Name:
Ajuga iva

Flowering period:
January to June

Status:
Frequent

Biotope:
Garrigue and disturbed ground

Notes:
Flowers can be yellow (refer to shades of yellow, p.150)

001 FRP This colour form is more common than the yellow flower

002 FRP Typical plant in coastal biotope

002 FRP Fleshy green leaves turning red

002 FRP Flowers are small but numerous

002 FRP

English:
Lesser Crystal-plant

Maltese:
Kristallina Komuni

Scientific Name:
Mesembryanthemum nodiflorum

Flowering period:
April to July

Status:
Common

Biotope:
Sandy patches and also on rocks near the sea

Notes:
Plant turns deep red in summer. Flowers 1cm with white petals

003 FRP

English:
Red Campion

Maltese:
Lsien l-Għasfur

Scientific Name:
Silene colorata

Flowering period:
November to June

Status:
Very common

Biotope:
Has adapted to many types of biotopes

Notes:
2cm flowers. Cannot be missed, adding a touch of colour wherever it is found

003 FRP The Red Campion can be found in large numbers when the conditions are right

003 FRP Flower detail

004 FRP The Italian Fumitory has the largest flowers in the family, reaching 1.5 cm

004 FRP

English:
Italian Fumitory

Maltese:
Daħnet l-Art Kbira

Scientific Name:
Fumaria gaillardotti

Flowering period:
December to May

Status:
Common

Biotope:
Farmland, road verges and also in valleys

Notes:
Various species to be found, with varying flower lengths. Flowers vary from 6mm to 15mm

005 FRP The stamens are important in the identification of Poppy species

005 FRP The bright red petals with a black mark at the bottom are characteristic of the Common Poppy

005 FRP A Poppy field

005 FRP

English:
Common Poppy

Maltese:
Pepprin

Scientific Name:
Papaver rhoeas

Flowering period:
March to May

Status:
Very Common

Biotope:
Mostly in fields, sometimes in very large numbers

Notes:
Various species of Poppies are to be found, all common, identified from the different colours and shapes of the stamens

005 FRP The small Bristly Poppy *Papaver hybridum*

005 FRP Fruit pods

006 FRP

English:
Sea-heath

Maltese:
Erba Franka

Scientific Name:
Frankenia hirsuta

Flowering period:
February to June

Status:
Common

Biotope:
Maritime rocks, sandy soil and sand

Notes:
Forms dense hairy mats. Flowers 1cm, pale violet or white

006 FRP Each plant carries large numbers of the small flowers

007 FRP Plant profile

007 FRP Flower detail

007 FRP

English:
Blue Stonecrop

Maltese:
Beżżul il-Baqra

Scientific Name:
Sedum caeruleum

Flowering period:
March to May

Status:
Common

Biotope:
Garrigue, rocky steppes and valleys

Notes:
Fleshy red leaves, growing mostly where puddles form in winter, forming low 3-15cm high mats with pinkish 1 cm flowers

008 FRP

English:
Narrow Navelwort

Maltese:
Żokret l-Għaġuża

Scientific Name:
Umbilicus horizontalis

Flowering period:
April to May

Status:
Frequent, but localized

Biotope:
Garrigue, mostly in shady crevices and depressions in rocks

Notes:
A Mediterranean species, not commonly met with, but found in good numbers where present

008 FRP The leaves are fleshy, very much like those of succulents

009 FRP Used to be grown as fodder

009 FRP

English:
Common Vetch

Maltese:
Ġilbiena Sewda

Scientific Name:
Vicia sativa

Flowering period:
February to May

Status:
Common

Biotope:
Mostly in disturbed environments, including fields

Notes:
Some similar subspecies. Grown as fodder. Found throughout Europe and North Africa

010 FRP The dual colouration of the Crimson Pea flower

010 FRP

English:
Crimson Pea

Maltese:
Ġilbiena tas-Serp

Scientific Name:
Lathyrus clymenum

Flowering period:
February to May

Status:
common

Biotope:
Mostly in valleys and disturbed ground

Notes:
A plant of the Mediterranean region

011 FRP

English:
Reversed Clover

Maltese:
Xnejn

Scientific Name:
Trifolium resupinatum

Flowering period:
April to June

Status:
Common

Biotope:
Mostly in damp valleys, but also on rocky ground

Notes:
Stems up to 30 cm long. Grows low on the ground, usually in places that would have held water in winter

011 FRP This plant usually grows low on the ground

011 FRP Flower close-up

012 FRP The crimson colour of the Winged Pea

012 FRP

English:
Winged Pea

Maltese:
Fiġġiela Ħamra

Scientific Name:
Lotus tetragonolobus

Flowering period:
February to May

Status:
Common

Biotope:
Garrigue, but also in valleys and disturbed terrain

Notes:
Flowers usually solitary. Found in Southern Europe, Western Asia and North Africa

013 FRP

English:
Star Clover

Maltese:
Xnien ta' l-Istilla

Scientific Name:
Trifolium stellatum

Flowering period:
March to May

Status:
Common

Biotope:
Mostly in garrigue and steppe

Notes:
Low lying plant. Leaves hairy. Pink flowers. Sepals become carrying case for pod in the shape of a star

013 FRP The Star Clover is a common species

013 FRP Flower detail

014 FRP Flower close-up

014 FRP

English:
Common Kidney Vetch

Maltese:
Silla tal-Blat

Scientific Name:
Anthyllis vulneraria

Flowering period:
March to May

Status:
Frequent

Biotope:
Garrigue and rocky steppe

Notes:
Grows in arid rocky terrain, usually found sprawling on limestone

015 FRP A small and easily overlooked flower

015 FRP

English:
Glandular Storksbill

Maltese:
Moxt

Scientific Name:
Erodium malacoides

Flowering period:
January to April

Status:
Very Common

Biotope:
Disturbed ground, fields and valleys

Notes:
Other similar species occur (Refer to Shades of Blue & Violet, No.043)

016 FRP Flower close-up

016 FRP A familiar scene in the Maltese countryside

016 FRP

English:
Sulla

Maltese:
Silla

Scientific Name:
Hedysarum coronarium

Flowering period:
March to May

Status:
Very Common

Biotope:
Cultivated as fodder, but also grows wild in various biotopes

Notes:
A species of the Mediterranean region, and is a familiar sight in the Maltese countryside

017 FRP

English:
Common Mallow

Maltese:
Ħobbejża Komuni

Scientific Name:
Malva sylvestris

Flowering period:
February to May

Status:
Very Common

Biotope:
Disturbed ground, garrigue

Notes:
In some localities covers large areas, such as in abandoned fields. The intensity of the colour varies from a pale pink to a dark purple, as seen in the photos

017 FRP Pinkish flowers

017 FRP Purplish flowers

018 FRP A species of Mallow that is on the increase, due to its adaptability to disturbed and rural environments

018 FRP

English:
Tree Mallow

Maltese:
Ħobbejża tas-Siġra

Scientific Name:
Lavatera arborea

Flowering period:
March to June

Status:
Frequent

Biotope:
Rocky coast and disturbed ground

Notes:
Can be 3 meters high with large flowers in clusters. Seems to be spreading

019 FRP Usually found in good numbers

019 FRP Flower detail of the Large Flowered Mallow

019 FRP Flowers can be up to 10 cm across

019 FRP

English:
Large Flowered Mallow

Maltese:
Ħobbejża tal-Warda Kbira

Scientific Name:
Lavatera trimestris

Flowering period:
April to July

Status:
Frequent

Biotope:
Steppic environments, clay slopes and country paths

Notes:
Pink flowers with darker veins could be from 7cm to 10cm across, offering a real spectacle where present in sufficient numbers

020 FRP Typical bush of the Hoary Rock-rose

020 FRP Flowers are up to 6 cm in diameter

020 FRP   Flower profile

020 FRP

English:
Hoary Rock-rose

Maltese:
Ċistu Roża

Scientific Name:
Cistus creticus

Flowering period:
March to May

Status:
Localized and rare

Biotope:
Garrigue and arid rocky areas

Notes:
In some localities it is the dominant species. The few localities where this species is found should be protected

020 FRP Leaves of Hoary Rock-rose

021 FRP Red leaves of the Cranesbill

021 FRP Flower close-up

021 FRP

English:
Cranesbill

Maltese:
Ġeranju

Scientific Name:
Geranium purpureum

Flowering period:
February to May

Status:
Frequent

Biotope:
Valleys and sheltered rocky areas

Notes:
These plants tend to like damp situations. A characteristic of this species are the palmate leaves which can be a vivid red. Similar species are to be found, identified mostly from the shape of their leaves and seed pods

022 FRP Flowering on erect stems

022 FRP Creeping, hence the name

022 FRP

English:
Creeping Loosestrife

Maltese:
Litrum ta' l-Ilma

Scientific Name:
Lythrum junceum

Flowering period:
April to June

Status:
Localized but frequent

Biotope:
Watercourses and damp places

Notes:
A plant that spreads by rhizomes and grows mostly, but not always, as a low creeping plant, hence the name. Branches up to 70cm in length

022 FRP Flower close-up

023 FRP

English:
Stinking Madder

Maltese:
Robbja

Scientific Name:
Putoria calabrica

Flowering period:
May to June

Status:
Rare

Biotope:
Garrigue and rocky valleys

Notes:
Can form mats of about 1 meter in diameter. A plant of the Mediterranean region

023 FRP The small trumpet like flowers of the Stinking Madder

024 FRP The most common colour type of the Scarlet Pimpernel

024 FRP Less common salmon pink colour

024 FRP

English:
Scarlet Pimpernel

Maltese:
Ħarira Ħamra

Scientific Name:
Anagallis arvensis

Flowering period:
February to July

Status:
Very common

Biotope:
Has adapted to a variety of environmental situations

Notes:
Two main colour varieties occur, One Blue (see shades of Blue and Violet section), and one Red, with different tones of pinks in between

024 FRP Rare pink background colour suffused with blue

025 FRP

English:
Mediterranean Heath

Maltese:
Erika

Scientific Name:
Erica multiflora

Flowering period:
December to May

Status:
Common

Biotope:
Karstic terrain including garrigue, rocky hillsides and upper valley sides

Notes:
Erect shrub, with short needle like leaves and dense clusters of pink elongate flowers. Dominant species in some localities

025 FRP Close-up of clusters of flowers of the Mediterranean Heath

026 FRP Flower head borne on stem

026 FRP

English:
Southern Scabious

Maltese:
Skabjoża

Scientific Name:
Scabiosa maritima

Flowering period:
May to August

Status:
Common

Biotope:
Has adapted to various different biotopes

Notes:
The single flower is borne on a stem 20cm to 60cm high

026 FRP Detail of pink flowerhead

027 FRP

English:
Mallow Bindweed

Maltese:
Leblieb tax-Xagħri

Scientific Name:
Convolvulus althaeoides

Flowering period:
March to June

Status:
Common

Biotope:
Mostly garrigue, but also disturbed ground and stone walls

Notes:
The dark center is a characteristic of this species

027 FRP The Mallow Bindweed sometimes grows as a climber

028 FRP Typical plant with multiple flowers

028 FRP Flower detail

028 FRP

English:
Common Centaury

Maltese:
Ċentawrja Kbira

Scientific Name:
Centaurium erythraea

Flowering period:
April to June

Status:
Common

Biotope:
Garrigue, rocky steppe and clay slopes

Notes:
Four species of Centaurium are found in Malta. The species also occurs in most of Europe and the Mediterranean region

029 FRP

English:
Slender Bindweed

Maltese:
Leblieb tax-Xagħri Ċar

Scientific Name:
Convolvulus elegantissimus

Flowering period:
March to June

Status:
Common

Biotope:
Garrigue and maquis

Notes:
Similar to Mallow Bindweed, but with the center of the flower white

029 FRP The slender Bindweed is usually found as a dense shrub producing many flowers

029 FRP The centre of the flower is always white

030 FRP Flower close-up showing the white and pink stripes

030 FRP

English:
Field Bindweed

Maltese:
Leblieb tar-Raba'

Scientific Name:
Convolvulus arvensis

Flowering period:
March to October

Status:
Very common

Biotope:
Cultivated and disturbed ground

Notes:
Flowers usually striped white and pink. Found all over Europe

031 FRP Flower detail

031 FRP

English:
Greater Snapdragon

Maltese:
Papoċċi Ħamra

Scientific Name:
Antirrhinum tortuosum

Flowering period:
All year

Status:
Very Common

Biotope:
Disturbed ground, rubble walls and valleys

Notes:
Of Mediterranean origin. Can be spectacular when found in large numbers due to its large size

031 FRP Greater Snapdragons

031 FRP The not so common pink variety of the Greater Snapdragon

032 FRP

English:
Pale Bugloss

Maltese:
Lsien il-Fart Abjad

Scientific Name:
Echium italicum

Flowering period:
April to June

Status:
Frequent

Biotope:
Valleys and disturbed ground

Notes:
A Hairy plant with an erect main stem and a number of horizontal branches usually with pinkish and bluish, flowers. Resembles a Christmas tree

032 FRP Leaves forming flat rosette at soil level

032 FRP Flower close-up

032 FRP The multi branched hairy erect stem

033 FRP The red slender stems of the parasitic Dodder

033 FRP

English:
Dodder

Maltese:
Pittma

Scientific Name:
Cuscuta epithymum

Flowering period:
March to April

Status:
Frequent

Biotope:
Garrigue and steppe

Notes:
A leafless parasitic plant forming a mat of red and slender stems on shrubs such as Thyme and Maltese Spurge. The pinkish flowers are small

033 FRP The minute flowers are pink

034 FRP

English:
Lesser Snapdragon

Maltese:
Papoċċ Irqiqa

Scientific Name:
Misopates orontium

Flowering period:
March to June

Status:
Localised but frequent

Biotope:
Mostly disused fields and disturbed ground

Notes:
Found in most of Europe and the Mediterranean region

034 FRP These flowers are so small they can easily be overlooked

034 FRP Flower detail

035 FRP

English:
Bellardia

Maltese:
Perlina Bajda

Scientific Name:
Bellardia trixago

Flowering period:
April to May

Status:
Frequent

Biotope:
Garrigue, steppes and also disturbed ground

Notes:
A semi parasitic plant on the roots of certain grasses

035 FRP Close-up of Bellardia

036 FRP

English:
Horn-of-plenty

Maltese:
Sieq il-Ħamiema

Scientific Name:
Fedia cornucopiae

Flowering period:
January to May

Status:
Common

Biotope:
Garrigue, steppe and valleys

Notes:
Usually single plants in garrigue, but in larger numbers in valleys

036 FRP Plant showing leaves

036 FRP Flower detail

037 FRP

English:
Rosy Garlic

Maltese:
Tewm Ħamrani

Scientific Name:
Allium roseum

Flowering period:
March to April

Status:
Frequent

Biotope:
Rocky terrain, including garrigue

Notes:
Flowers can be whitish to dark pink, borne on 30cm stem. A Mediterranean species

037 FRP Flower head borne on stem

037 FRP Flower close-up

038 FRP Red Dock growing on a substrate of sand

038 FRP

English:
Red Dock

Maltese:
Qarsajja

Scientific Name:
Rumex bucephalophorus

Flowering period:
December to May

Status:
Localised but not rare

Biotope:
Garrigue and in sandy bays

Notes:
Grows to a height of 35 cm with very small flowers

039 FRP

English:
Field Gladiolus

Maltese:
Ħabb il-Qamħ

Scientific Name:
Gladiolus italicus

Flowering period:
March to May

Status:
Common

Biotope:
Disturbed ground and cultivated fields

Notes:
A common species in the Mediterranean region

039 FRP Field Gladiolus

039 FRP Newly developed green seed pods

039 FRP Seed pods turned brown

039 FRP Seed pods bursting open

040 FRP Several similar species of Clustered Dock can be found on the Islands

040 FRP

English:
Clustered Dock

Maltese:
Qarsajja ta' l-Ilma

Scientific Name:
Rumex conglomeratus

Flowering period:
April to June

Status:
Common

Biotope:
Damp valleys and along watercourses

Notes:
Up to 90 cm high, with small flowers clustered around branches of inflorescences

041 FRP

English:
Southern Squinancywort

Maltese:
—

Scientific Name:
Asperula aristata

Flowering period:
February to June

Status:
Common

Biotope:
Garrigue

Notes:
A species of the Mediterranean region

041 FRP The colour intensity of the flowers varies

042 FRP Each plant can carry numerous flowers

042 FRP

English:
Brown Figwort

Maltese:
Nittiena

Scientific Name:
Scrophularia peregrina

Flowering period:
March to May

Status:
Common

Biotope:
Shaded and damp places, including waste ground

Notes:
An annual of the Mediterranean region, with very small flowers

042 FRP Close-up of the minute flowers

043 FRP The flowers are very small, a few mm across

043 FRP

English:
Hairy Catchfly

Maltese:
Lsien l-Għasfur irqiq

Scientific Name:
Silene sedoides

Flowering period:
March to May

Status:
Frequent

Biotope:
Coastal rocks and sandy patches

Notes:
Very small flower. Mediterranean region, nearly always on Islands

043 FRP The leaves are very fleshy, succulent like

044 FRP One of the smaller Centaury species with a white center

044 FRP

English:
Lesser Centaury

Maltese:
Ċentawrija żgħira

Scientific Name:
Centaurium pulchellum

Flowering period:
April to June

Status:
Frequent

Biotope:
Garrigue and coastal rocky steppe

Notes:
Stem only 15 cm high. Flowers smaller than that of the Common Centaury *C.erythraea*

045 FRP Branched stem bears many flowers

045 FRP Plant growing out of water in a watercourse

045 FRP Flower close-up

045 FRP

English:
Water Plantain

Maltese:
Biżbula ta' l-ilma

Scientific Name:
Alisma plantago-aquatica

Flowering period:
May to August

Status:
Frequent but requires specialized conditions

Biotope:
Watercourses

Notes:
Can be as high as two meters, with a stout stem

046 FRP

English:
Mediterranean Mallow

Maltese:
Ħobbejża tat-toroq

Scientific Name:
Malva cretica

Flowering period:
March to June

Status:
Frequent

Biotope:
Arid disturbed ground, roadsides and fields

Notes:
Erect stem up to 40 cm high. A species of the Mediterranean region

046 FRP Flower detail

047 FRP Woody Sandwort close-up

047 FRP Individual plants can carry numerous flowers

047 FRP

English:
Woody Sandwort

Maltese:
Ramlina Għawdxija

Scientific Name:
Rhodalsine geniculata

Flowering period:
April to June

Status:
Rare in Malta, frequent in Gozo

Biotope:
Cliffs, coastal sandy areas

Notes:
Stems up to 30 cm high, woody at the base. A species of the Mediterranean region

048 FRP

English:
Clustered Sulla

Maltese:
Silla salvaġġa

Scientific Name:
Hedysarum glomeratum

Flowering period:
March to May

Status:
Scarce

Biotope:
Garrigue and coastal steppes

Notes:
Stems up to 40 cm long, usually growing flat on the ground

048 FRP The stems growing flat on the ground

048 FRP Flower detail

049 FRP The plant usually has an orange tinge due to the stems that are drying

049 FRP

English:
Slender Centaury

Maltese:
Ċentawrija rqieqa

Scientific Name:
Centaurium tenuifolium

Flowering period:
April to July

Status:
Common

Biotope:
Clay slopes and grass-steppe

Notes:
Stem up to 25 cm high. Found along the Atlantic coast, Mediterranean into Asia Minor

Shades of Blue and Violet

001 FBV Typical plant and Biotope

001 FBV

English:
Maltese Stocks

Maltese:
Ġiżi ta' Malta

Scientific Name:
Matthiola incana ssp.melitensis

Flowering period:
February to May

Status:
Very rare in Malta, localised but more frequent in Gozo

Biotope:
Coastal cliffs

Notes:
An endemic species, described as recently as 1988

001 FBV Maltese Stocks flowers and buds

001 FBV Flower detail

001 FBV Leaves of Maltese Stocks

002 FBV

English:
Crown Anemone

Maltese:
Kaħwiela

Scientific Name:
Anemone coronaria

Flowering period:
January to March

Status:
Frequent

Biotope:
Maquis and garrigue, but also in disturbed ground

Notes:
A flower of the Mediterranean region

002 FBV The Crown Anemone is met with in winter

003 FBV Flower close-up

003 FBV The elongated inflorescence

003 FBV

English:
Winged Larkspur

Maltese:
Sieq il-Ħamiema Vjola

Scientific Name:
Delphinium halteratum

Flowering period:
May to September

Status:
Scarce

Biotope:
Disturbed ground and road verges

Notes:
Forms an inflorescence up to 70cm high

004 FBV Opium Poppy

004 FBV Flower detail

004 FBV

English:
Opium Poppy

Maltese:
Xaħxieħ Vjola

Scientific Name:
Papaver setigerum

Flowering period:
February to May

Status:
Common

Biotope:
Mostly disturbed urban areas

Notes:
Cultivated since ancient times, probably introduced

004 FBV Light coloured form

005 FBV Typical plants in their natural habitat

005 FBV Close-up showing whitish hairy leaves

005 FBV Flower detail, also showing the elongate siliqua or fruit ending in three stiff horns, a characteristic of the species

005 FBV

English:
Mediterranean Stocks

Maltese:
Ġiżi tal-Baħar

Scientific Name:
Matthiola tricuspidata

Flowering period:
March to May

Status:
Frequent

Biotope:
Coastal sandy areas

Notes:
Said to be spreading and less rare than in previous times
A species found across the Mediterranean region

006 FBV Inflorescence with flowers

006 FBV Flower detail

006 FBV

English:
Sea Rocket

Maltese:
Kromb il-Baħar

Scientific Name:
Cakile maritima

Flowering period:
December to August

Status:
Frequent

Biotope:
Sand dunes and other sandy environments

Notes:
Flowers can be violet, pink or white, plant can reach height of 60 cm

006 FBV The fleshy leaves

007 FBV

English:
Pitch Clover

Maltese:
Silla tal-Mogħoż

Scientific Name:
Psoralea bituminosa

Flowering period:
February to May

Status:
Very common

Biotope:
Found in most habitat-types

Notes:
When crushed, the leaves emit a smell like that of pitch

007 FBV When conditions are right each flowering plant produces many flowers

007 FBV Flower close-up

008 FBV The prostrate stems are reddish

008 FBV

English:
Hyssop Loosestrife

Maltese:
Litrum ta' l-Ghadajjar

Scientific Name:
Lythrum hyssopifolia

Flowering period:
April to May

Status:
Frequent but localised

Biotope:
Rock pools on karstland

Notes:
Flowers to be found when rock pools dry up

008 FBV The flowers are smaller than those of the Creeping Loosestrife

009 FBV

English:
Field Madder

Maltese:
Ħarxajja Roża

Scientific Name:
Sherardia arvensis

Flowering period:
February to May

Status:
Common

Biotope:
In a variety of biotopes, garrigue, steppes and disturbed ground

Notes:
Found throughout Europe, North Africa into Western Asia

009 FBV The Field Madder produces very small flowers in bunches

010 FBV Flower detail of the Maltese Sea-lavender

010 FBV The flowers are small but numerous

010 FBV

English:
Maltese Sea-lavender

Maltese:
Limonju ta' Malta

Scientific Name:
Limonium melitensis

Flowering period:
July to September

Status:
Common

Biotope:
Coastal areas ,cliffs and clay slopes

Notes:
An endemic species. Other similar species are to be found, with slight differences in stems and branches

011 FBV

English:
Blue Pimpernel

Maltese:
Ħarira Kaħla

Scientific Name:
Anagallis arvensis

Flowering period:
February to July

Status:
Very common

Biotope:
In a variety of biotopes, from garrigue to disturbed ground

Notes:
Many different colours (see also shades of red and pink)

011 FBV An early flower, coming into bloom as early February

011 FBV Flower detail

012 FBV Blue flower

012 FBV

English:
Small-Flowered Bugloss

Maltese:
Lsien il-Fart Żgħir

Scientific Name:
Echium parviflorum

Flowering period:
January to June

Status:
Very common

Biotope:
Found in a variety of biotopes

Notes:
Flowers on the same plant can be pink or blue. Leaves bristly

012 FBV Pink flower

013 FBV The stem and leaves of the Large Blue Alkanet are hairy

013 FBV Flowers – a close-up

013 FBV

English:
Large Blue Alkanet

Maltese:
Lsien il-Fart Ikħal

Scientific Name:
Anchusa azurea

Flowering period:
March to July

Status:
Frequent, but localised

Biotope:
Clayey soils and disturbed ground

Notes:
Plant with rigid erect stems, up to 150 cm high. Leaves covered with bristles

013 FBV Different colour form – in this case one specimen out of a total of circa fifty plants in one area

014 FBV Rarer pink flower of the Borage

014 FBV Usual blue colour

014 FBV

English:
Borage

Maltese:
Fidloqqom

Scientific Name:
Borago officinalis

Flowering period:
January to May

Status:
Common

Biotope:
Most habitat-types, growing everywhere

Notes:
Branched robust plant can be up to 70 cm high. Leaves and stems covered with bristles. Rarely with pink flowers

015 FBV Showing hairiness of plant

015 FBV Pink and purple flowers on the same plant

015 FBV Dark veins on the flower

015 FBV

English:
Blue Hound's-tongue

Maltese:
Lsien il-Kelb

Scientific Name:
Cynoglossum creticum

Flowering period:
February to May

Status:
Frequent

Biotope:
Valleys and disturbed ground

Notes:
Flowers can be pink or purple on the same plant. Leaves are hairy

016 FBV Large shrub with numerous flowers

016 FBV Leaves

016 FBV Flower detail

016 FBV

English:
Chaste Tree

Maltese:
Siġra tal-Virgi

Scientific Name:
Vitex agnus-castus

Flowering period:
May to September

Status:
Scarce and localised

Biotope:
Watercourses; more frequent in Gozo

Notes:
Large shrub 200 to 300 cm high. Leaves fragrant. Flowers can be bluish, pink or rarely white. Stems used in traditional basket making for handles and bases

017 FBV Violet flowers of the Olive-leaved Germander

017 FBV

English:
Olive-leaved Germander

Maltese:
Żebbuġija

Scientific Name:
Teucrium fruticans

Flowering period:
January to June

Status:
Common

Biotope:
Garrigue, maquis and rocky valley banks

Notes:
Forms a dense shrub, usually the dominant species in the locality. Flowers can be white or violet

017 FBV Olive-leaved Germander flowers are usually found in pairs

018 FBV Mediterranean Thyme shrub in typical habitat

018 FBV Some shrubs produce Whitish flowers

018 FBV Flower detail

018 FBV

English:
Mediterranean Thyme

Maltese:
Saghtar

Scientific Name:
Thymbra capitata

Flowering period:
May to August

Status:
Common

Biotope:
Garrigue

Notes:
Forms a dense woody shrub, up to 100 cm high. Leaves very aromatic. Often the only greenery in garrigue during the hot months

018 FBV Honey bee feeding on thyme, resulting in the famous local Malta Honey

019 FBV Flower detail

019 FBV

English:
Blue Broomrape

Maltese:
Budebbus Ikħal

Scientific Name:
Orobanche lavandulacea

Flowering period:
March to May

Status:
Frequent

Biotope:
Garrigue, but also disturbed ground including fields

Notes:
Parasitic on Broad Beans and on *Dittrichia viscosa*

019 FBV Stem of Blue broomrape

020 FBV Each flower is only a few mm across

020 FBV

English:
Vervain

Maltese:
Buqexrem

Scientific Name:
Verbena officinalis

Flowering period:
April to December

Status:
Common

Biotope:
Disturbed ground

Notes:
Long erect stalks up to 100 cm bearing small flowers

021 FBV Leaves of the Water Speedwell

021 FBV Flower close-up

021 FBV

English:
Water Speedwell

Maltese:
Veronika ta' l-Ilma

Scientific Name:
Veronica anagallis-aquatica

Flowering period:
March to October

Status:
Frequent

Biotope:
Watercourses

Notes:
Erect stem up to 100 cm high. Almost cosmopolitan

022 FBV The fleshy leaves

022 FBV Plant in its typical habitat

022 FBV Flower close-up

022 FBV

English:
Maltese Rock-centaury

Maltese:
Widnet il-Baħar

Scientific Name:
Palaeocyanus crassifolius

Flowering period:
May to July

Status:
Scarce in the wild

Biotope:
Cliffs

Notes:
The national plant. An endemic species. It is being cultivated and grown in gardens and used in road embellishment, but nothing beats seeing it in the natural habitat, our majestic cliffs

023 FBV Spiny shrub

023 FBV Flowers are to be found only in the early morning

023 FBV Flower detail

023 FBV

English:
Spiny Chicory

Maltese:
Qanfuda

Scientific Name:
Cichorium spinosum

Flowering period:
May to July

Status:
Frequent

Biotope:
Coastal rocky terrain

Notes:
Forms into a small ball shape shrub with spiny branches, very much like a hedgehog, hence the Maltese name. The flowers open only in the early hours of the morning

024 FBV

English:
Pennyroyal

Maltese:
Plejju

Scientific Name:
Mentha pulegium

Flowering period:
May to August

Status:
Common

Biotope:
Damp valley-beds and in silted rock pools

Notes:
Strong smell of mint when leaves are crushed. Stem up to 40 cm, supporting dense bunches of small flowers

024 FBV Under favorable conditions the plant can be plentiful

024 FBV Flower close-up

025 FBV

English:
Maltese Savory

Maltese:
Xpakkapietra

Scientific Name:
Micromeria microphylla

Flowering period:
January to July

Status:
Common

Biotope:
Garrigue, rocky steppe and valley sides

Notes:
Widely used as a medicinal plant especially for gallstones

025 FBV This species forms very small shrublets, with small flowers

026 FBV Flower showing the long involucral bracts

026 FBV

English:
Smooth Goatsbeard

Maltese:
Leħjet il-Bodbod

Scientific Name:
Tragopogon hybridus

Flowering period:
April to May

Status:
Scarce

Biotope:
Abandoned fields especially with clayey soil

Notes:
Plant up to 80 cm high, with grass like leaves.
Mediterranean region

026 FBV Flower detail

026 FBV Flower detail

026 FBV Leaves and fruiting heads of the Smooth Goatsbeard

027 FBV

English:
Chicory

Maltese:
Ċikwejra

Scientific Name:
Cichorium intybus

Flowering period:
May to October

Status:
Frequent

Biotope:
Mostly on disturbed terrain

Notes:
Unlike the Spiny Chicory, the flowers of this species are borne along the length of the rigid erect stems that can be up to 120 cm high

027 FBV Flower on stalk

027 FBV Flower detail

028 FBV Common colour form of the Cretan Mallow

028 FBV

English:
Cretan Mallow

Maltese:
Ħobbejża Wieqfa

Scientific Name:
Lavatera cretica

Flowering period:
February to May

Status:
Common

Biotope:
Disturbed terrain, including cultivated fields

Notes:
Flowers in clusters of up to 3 flowers. An erect plant, growing to more than 200 cm

029 FBV

English:
Flax

Maltese:
Kittien

Scientific Name:
Linum usitatissimum

Flowering period:
April to May

Status:
Rare

Biotope:
Garrigue and also sandy shores

Notes:
Erect stem up to 60 cm high, usually branched. Found in the Mediterranean region and Western Europe

029 FBV The pale blue colour of this species is unusual

029 FBV Flower close-up

030 FBV Early stages of flower bearing head

030 FBV

English:
Sicilian Squill

Maltese:
Għansar Ikħal

Scientific Name:
Scilla sicula

Flowering period:
March to April

Status:
Scarce

Biotope:
Mostly in valleys, but also within karstic terrain

Notes:
Endemic to Malta, Sicily and Calabria, but nowhere common

030 FBV Flower detail of the Sicilian Squill

030 FBV Well developed head with numerous flowers

030 FBV Flower head on single spike

031 FBV

English:
Tassel Hyacinth

Maltese:
Basal il-Ħnieżer

Scientific Name:
Muscari comosum

Flowering period:
March to May

Status:
Common

Biotope:
Steppes and disturbed ground such as fallow fields

Notes:
Mediterranean region, Central and Eastern Europe

031 FBV The Tassel Hyacinth is a bulbous plant

031 FBV The stem (called a scape) bearing the flowers can be up to 45 cm high

031 FBV The flowers borne by the scape are numerous

032 FBV Florets close-up

032 FBV

English:
Wild Leek

Maltese:
Kurrat Salvaġġ

Scientific Name:
Allium commutatum

Flowering period:
April to June

Status:
Common

Biotope:
Rocky terrain and disturbed ground

Notes:
Up to 100 cm high. Spherical inflorescence with numerous small flowers

032 FBV Wild Leek inflorescence

033 FBV Umbels with developing flowers

033 FBV

English:
Maltese Leek

Maltese:
Kurrat ta' Malta

Scientific Name:
Allium melitense

Flowering period:
April to June

Status:
Common

Biotope:
Coastal rocky areas

Notes:
Differs from the Wild Leek in being only about 25 cm high. Said to be endemic

033 FBV Close-up of umbel of Maltese Leek

033 FBV Flower close-up

034 FBV Typical group of flowers

034 FBV Flower detail

034 FBV

English:
Barbary Nut Iris

Maltese:
Fjurdulis Salvaġġ

Scientific Name:
Gynandriris sisyrinchium

Flowering period:
March to May

Status:
Common

Biotope:
Arid rocky ground and soil-covered footpaths

Notes:
Bulbous. Flowers open in the afternoon, closing at dusk. Rarely more than 8 to 12 cm high

035 FBV

English:
Vipers-bugloss

Maltese:
Lsien il-Fart

Scientific Name:
Echium sabulicola

Flowering period:
March to May

Status:
Rare

Biotope:
Coastal areas

Notes:
A Mediterranean species, extending to central Europe and Asia

035 FBV The deep purple colour and slightly larger flowers distinguishes this species from the commoner Small-flowered Bugloss

036 FBV The species is in leaf all year round

036 FBV Flower detail

036 FBV

English:
Southern Dwarf Iris

Maltese:
Bellus

Scientific Name:
Iris pseudopumila

Flowering period:
February to May

Status:
Rare

Biotope:
Rocky steppe and garrigue

Notes:
The colour of different populations of this species can either be a deep violet or white to pale yellow

037 FBV The stems of the Sicilian Iris are usually branched

037 FBV Flower detail

037 FBV

English:
Sicilian Iris

Maltese:
Fjurdulis Sqalli

Scientific Name:
Iris sicula

Flowering period:
April to June

Status:
Very rare

Biotope:
Rocky terrain and maquis

Notes:
Can reach a height of 120 cm. Endemic to Sicily and Malta

038 FBV Showing the slender leaves

038 FBV A whitish specimen

038 FBV

English:
Sand-crocus

Maltese:
Żagħfran tal-Blat

Scientific Name:
Romulea ramiflora

Flowering period:
February to April

Status:
Common

Biotope:
Steppe and garrigue

Notes:
Another three species are recorded from Malta, including an endemic

038 FBV Flower close-up

039 FBV

English:
Bean Broomrape

Maltese:
Budebbus tal-Ful

Scientific Name:
Orobanche crenata

Flowering period:
March to May

Status:
Common

Biotope:
Disturbed ground including fields

Notes:
Parasitic on Broad Bean. Largest species of Broomrape in the Maltese Islands

039 FBV Can be commonly seen in fields growing next to Broad Bean plantations

040 FBV Flower close-up

040 FBV

English:
Square-stalked Willowherb

Maltese:
—

Scientific Name:
Epilobium tetragonum

Flowering period:
April to October

Status:
Scarce

Biotope:
Damp valleys and along water courses

Notes:
Stems up to 110 cm high. Found in most of Europe into Western Asia

040 FBV Inflorescence

041 FBV Autumn Grape Hyacinth has less flowers than the Tassel Hyacinth

041 FBV

English:
Autumn Grape Hyacinth

Maltese:
Ġjaċint tal-Ħarifa

Scientific Name:
Muscari parviflorum

Flowering period:
September to October

Status:
Frequent

Biotope:
Garrigue

Notes:
This flower always appears after the first rains

042 FBV

English:
Common Freesia

Maltese:
Friżja

Scientific Name:
Freesia refracta

Flowering period:
March to April

Status:
Frequent

Biotope:
Valleys and woodland

Notes:
A native of South Africa, but has become naturalized

042 FBV The Common Freesia is an alien species

043 FBV

English:
Sand Storksbill

Maltese:
Miskta tar-Ramel

Scientific Name:
Erodium laciniatum

Flowering period:
February to June

Status:
Rare and vulnerable

Biotope:
Sand dunes

Notes:
The beak-like fruit (hence the name) can be up to 90 mm long, a distinguishing feature as all beaks are shorter in the other related and similar species

043 FBV Flower detail

043 FBV Plant showing the beaks produced by the Sand Storkbill

044 FBV Showing the slender trailing stem of the Blue Bindweed

044 FBV Flower close-up

044 FBV

English:
Blue Bindweed

Maltese:
Leblieb tal-werqa tleqq

Scientific Name:
Convolvulus siculus

Flowering period:
March to June

Status:
Scarce

Biotope:
Disturbed ground and abandoned fields

Notes:
Stems up to 60 cm long, usually trailing, sometimes twining. A species from the Mediterranean region and Atlantic Islands

045 FBV

English:
Ivy-leaved Toadflax

Maltese:
—

Scientific Name:
Cymbalaria muralis

Flowering period:
February to May

Status:
Scarce

Biotope:
Shady walls, valleys and gardens

Notes:
Listed as rare in older publications, but seems to be on the increase in certain localities

045 FBV The leaves resemble those of the Ivy, on a smaller scale

046 FBV Grows into a sizeable bush, with the flowers borne on erect stems

046 FBV

English:
Mediterranean Restharrow

Maltese:
—

Scientific Name:
Ononis mitissima

Flowering period:
April to July

Status:
Scarce

Biotope:
Sandy and clayey soil, sometimes on disturbed ground

Notes:
Erect stems up to 60 cm high. A species of the Mediterranean region

Orchids

001 FO Early stages of flower

001 FO

English:
Common Pyramidal Orchid

Maltese:
Orkida Piramidali

Scientific Name:
Anacamptis pyramidalis

Flowering period:
April and May

Status:
Common

Biotope:
Garrigue, maquis, steppic terrain and even abandoned fields

Notes:
Stem can be 50 cm high. Colour usually an intense violet pink, when compared to the much paler Maltese Pyramidal Orchid. Has a wide distribution, from Europe to Central Russia, North Africa and Western Asia

001 FO Typical flowers of the Common Pyramidal Orchid

001 FO Flower close-up

002 FO Entire plant

002 FO Close-up of 'Tongue'

002 FO

English:
Small-flowered Tongue Orchid

Maltese:
Orkida ta' l-Ilsiena Żgħira

Scientific Name:
Serapias parviflora

Flowering period:
March to April

Status:
Frequent

Biotope:
Garrigue and rocky steppe

Notes:
Stem up to 25 cm high. A species of Western Europe and the Mediterranean region

003 FO Typical plant

003 FO Flower close-up

003 FO

English:
Brown Orchid

Maltese:
Dubbiena

Scientific Name:
Ophrys fusca

Flowering period:
December to May

Status:
Frequent

Biotope:
Garrigue and maquis

Notes:
Some authorities distinguish various races as separate species. Found only in the Mediterranean region

004 FO

English:
Mirror Orchid

Maltese:
Dubbiena Kahla

Scientific Name:
Ophrys speculum

Flowering period:
March and April

Status:
Rare

Biotope:
Garrigue

Notes:
Found more often in Gozo than in Malta

004 FO The labellum in this species is shiny, resembling the thorax of certain species of bees and wasps

004 FO The labellum is also encircled with short hairs, enhancing the mimicry even further

005 FO The markings on the Labellum vary. In this case there are 2 small silvery markings

005 FO This flower has markings resembling a complete horseshoe

005 FO

English:
Maltese Spider Orchid

Maltese:
Brimba Sewda

Scientific Name:
Ophrys sphegodes ssp. melitensis

Flowering period:
March and April

Status:
Rare

Biotope:
Garrigue, maquis and rocky steppes

Notes:
An endemic species. Very variable in its markings

005 FO In this flower, the markings resemble an incomplete horseshoe

006 FO

English:
Maltese Pyramidal Orchid

Maltese:
Orkida Piramidali ta' Malta

Scientific Name:
Anacamptis urvilleana

Flowering period:
February to April

Status:
Frequent

Biotope:
Garrigue and rocky steppe

Notes:
Flowers before the Common Pyramidal Orchid. The flowers are paler, sometimes nearly white (photo p.296) and usually smaller than that of the previous species. Endemic

006 FO It is common to find flowers of this species in groups of three or more

006 FO This species tends to produce flowers that are paler than those of the Common Pyramidal Orchid

006 FO Flower detail of the Maltese Pyramidal Orchid

007 FO The entire plant

007 FO Flower detail

007 FO

English:
Fan-lipped Orchid

Maltese:
Orkida Ħamra

Scientific Name:
Orchis collina

Flowering period:
January to March

Status:
Frequent

Biotope:
Garrigue and sometimes abandoned fields

Notes:
Stem up to 20 cm high. One of the earliest Orchids to be met with

008 FO

English:
Milky Orchid

Maltese:
Orkida tat-Tikek

Scientific Name:
Orchis conica

Flowering period:
December to March

Status:
Frequent

Biotope:
Garrigue, steppe and abandoned fields

Notes:
The colours and patterns of the flowers are very variable, as can be seen in the photos

008 FO This flower has dark maroon markings

008 FO Flower close-up

008 FO A flower with much paler colours

009 FO The entire plant

009 FO

English:
Scented Bug Orchid

Maltese:
Orkida Tfuħ

Scientific Name:
Orchis fragrans

Flowering period:
April to May

Status:
Frequent

Biotope:
Garrigue and abandoned fields

Notes:
Stem can be up to 30 cm high. Colour intensity varies. A species of the Mediterranean region

009 FO Flower detail of the Scented Bug Orchid

010 FO Entire plant

010 FO

English:
Bumble Bee Orchid

Maltese:
Naħla

Scientific Name:
Ophrys bombyliflora

Flowering period:
March and April

Status:
Frequent

Biotope:
Garrigue and rocky steppe

Notes:
This Orchid mimics a bee, complete with pollen sacks. Another species confined to the Mediterranean region

010 FO Flower close-up. Species from the genus Ophrys have flowers that mimic insects to attract pollinators

Shades of Green and Grasses

001 FG

English:
Maidenhair Fern

Maltese:
Tursin il-Bir

Scientific Name:
Adiantum capillus-veneris

Flowering period:
No Flowers

Status:
Frequent

Biotope:
Damp rocks in shaded valleys, walls of caves and wells

Notes:
Leaves can be up to 60 cm long

001 FG Picture of Maidenhair fern growing on the sides of an old well

002 FG

English:
Large-leaved Stinging Nettle

Maltese:
Ħurrieq Komuni

Scientific Name:
Urtica dubia

Flowering period:
November to May

Status:
Very common

Biotope:
Gardens, urban areas and sheltered valleys

Notes:
Up to 80 cm high. Leaves bear stinging hairs. Minute flowers are wind pollinated

002 FG The Stinging Nettles is the larval food plant of the Red Admiral, Vanessa atalanta

003 FG Typical shrub of the Shrubby Glasswort

003 FG Close-up of the Shrubby Glasswort

003 FG

English:
Shrubby Glasswort

Maltese:
Almeridja tal-Blat

Scientific Name:
Arthrocnemum macrostachyum

Flowering period:
July to November

Status:
Rare

Biotope:
Rocky coastal areas

Notes:
Shrub up to 100 cm high, becoming reddish on maturity

004 FG

English:
Pellitory-of-the-wall

Maltese:
Xeħt ir-Riħ

Scientific Name:
Parietaria judaica

Flowering period:
All year round

Status:
Very common everywhere

Biotope:
Along walls in urban and country habitats

Notes:
Flowers are very small. Stem sometimes reddish. All plant covered in hairs

004 FG The hairy Pellitory-of-the-wall

005 FG The fleshy leaves of the Sea Samphire

005 FG

English:
Sea Samphire

Maltese:
Bużbież il-Baħar

Scientific Name:
Crithmum maritimum

Flowering period:
June to September

Status:
Frequent

Biotope:
Rocky coasts

Notes:
Stems up to 35 cm high. Fleshy leaves. Widespread in the Mediterranean, Black Sea and the Atlantic coast of Europe

005 FG The big flower heads attract many insects in the hot and dry summer months

006 FG Leaves of none flowering branches are lobed

006 FG Leaves of flowering branches are simple

006 FG

English:
Ivy

Maltese:
Liedna

Scientific Name:
Hedera helix

Flowering period:
September to November

Status:
Frequent

Biotope:
Valley walls, maquis and large gardens

Notes:
A climber. Various cultivars exist, differing in size, shape and colour of leaves

006 FG Flowerheads

006 FG The fruit of the Ivy is an important food source for migrating birds

007 FG Toothed leaves

007 FG Small flowers on hairy inflorescences

007 FG

English:
Toothed Plantain

Maltese:
Biżbula tas-Snien

Scientific Name:
Plantago serraria

Flowering period:
March to June

Status:
Common

Biotope:
Valleys and disturbed sites

Notes:
Numerous short and thick stems. Widespread in the Mediterranean region

007 FG The similar species Buck's-horn Plantain (Biżbula tal-Baħar) *Plantago coronopus* has narrower fleshy leaves, is found in similar habitats

008 FG

English:
Hare's-foot Plantain

Maltese:
Biżbula Komuni

Scientific Name:
Plantago lagopus

Flowering period:
February to May

Status:
Very common

Biotope:
All types of habitats

Notes:
Stems up to 20 cm high

008 FG This very common species is found in a variety of habitats

009 FG The Greater Plantain is rather restricted because of its environmental needs (watercourses)

009 FG

English:
Greater Plantain

Maltese:
Biżbula Kbira

Scientific Name:
Plantago major

Flowering period:
March to November

Status:
Scarce

Biotope:
Along watercourses

Notes:
With large veined leaves

012 FG

English:
Sea Rush

Maltese:
Simar tal-Baħar

Scientific Name:
Bolboschoenus maritimus

Flowering period:
April to June

Status:
Rare

Biotope:
Watercourses and salt marshes

Notes:
Stems up to 100 cm long. A cosmopolitan species

012 FG Another species that needs salt marshes to thrive, the Sea Rush is not widespread and rare

013 FG This species is not as rare as the Sharp Rush

013 FG

English:
Round-headed Club-rush

Maltese:
Simar tal-Boċċi

Scientific Name:
Holoschoenus vulgaris

Flowering period:
April to July

Status:
Frequent

Biotope:
Watercourses and valley beds

Notes:
Flowers in bunches on the 100 cm stems

013 FG Flower close-up

014 FG Detail of the flower of the Sweet Galingale

014 FG

English:
Sweet Galingale

Maltese:
Bordi tal-Wied

Scientific Name:
Cyperus longus

Flowering period:
April to September

Status:
Frequent

Biotope:
Watercourses and damp valleys

Notes:
Similar species occur. A plant of the Mediterranean region

015 FG

English:
Sand Galingale

Maltese:
Bordi tar-Ramel

Scientific Name:
Cyperus capitatus

Flowering period:
March to September

Status:
Rare

Biotope:
Sand dunes

Notes:
Due to its specialised environmental requirements this is a highly threatened and vulnerable species, found only in a couple of locations

015 FG The leafy winged stems of the Sand Galingale

015 FG Flower detail

016 FG Since coastal salt marshes are rare the distribution of this species is restricted and becoming rarer

016 FG

English:
Sharp Rush

Maltese:
Simar Niggież

Scientific Name:
Juncus acutus

Flowering period:
March to May

Status:
Scarce

Biotope:
Coastal saltmarshes

Notes:
In decline and found only in a few localities. Needle like and sharply pointed leaves can be 150 cm long

017 FG

English:
Southern Reed-mace

Maltese:
Buda

Scientific Name:
Typha domingensis

Flowering period:
May to July

Status:
Scarce

Biotope:
Watercourses

Notes:
Stems can be up to 300 cm high

017 FG The inflorescence of the Southern Reed-mace

018 FG Typical patch of Goat grass

018 FG

English:
Goat Grass

Maltese:
Brimba

Scientific Name:
Aegilops geniculata

Flowering period:
March to June

Status:
Common

Biotope:
Steppe and garrigue

Notes:
Up to 20 cm high. Usually found forming large patches

019 FG The Cockscomb Grass, apart from being found in the Mediterranean region, is also found in Asia and is widely introduced in other regions

019 FG

English:
Cockscomb Grass

Maltese:
Deqquqa

Scientific Name:
Dactylis hispanica

Flowering period:
April to June

Status:
Common

Biotope:
Steppe and valleys

Notes:
Up to 100 cm high. A Mediterranean species

020 FG

English:
Animated Oat

Maltese:
Ħafur Kbir

Scientific Name:
Avena sterilis

Flowering period:
March to May

Status:
Very common

Biotope:
Various, preferring disturbed ground

Notes:
Can reach 100 cm in height. Various similar species occur

020 FG A species found growing practically everywhere

021 FG The Friar's Cowl is usually found growing in groups

021 FG

English:
Friar's Cowl

Maltese:
Garni tal-Pipi

Scientific Name:
Arisarum vulgare

Flowering period:
December to April

Status:
Very Common

Biotope:
Disturbed ground and damp valleys

Notes:
Up to 25 cm high. Sometimes found in large numbers. A species found throughout the Mediterranean region

021 FG Flower close-up

022 FG

English:
Fat Hen

Maltese:
Għobbejra Bajdanija

Scientific Name:
Chenopodium album

Flowering period:
June to October

Status:
Very common

Biotope:
Urban areas, roadsides, rubble and other disturbed areas

Notes:
Can be 150 cm high. The flowers are very small, growing in clusters. Probably introduced. Cosmopolitan

022 FG The leaves are variable, but usually lancet shaped

023 FG A common species in valleys that hold water

023 FG By late May the Annual Beard-grass has dried up

023 FG

English:
Annual Beard-grass

Maltese:
Denb il-Liebru Kbir

Scientific Name:
Polypogon monspeliensis

Flowering period:
March to May

Status:
Common

Biotope:
Damp valleys

Notes:
Stem up to 80 cm high. Widespread

024 FG

English:
Esparto Grass

Maltese:
Ħalfa

Scientific Name:
Lygeum spartum

Flowering period:
February to June

Status:
Common

Biotope:
Mainly grows on clay slopes near the sea

Notes:
Up to 75 cm tall. It helps bind the clay on which it grows, preventing erosion

024 FG Typical clump growing on clay

024 FG The spikelets are bracts holding the small flowers

025 FG Typical shrub

025 FG

English:
Maltese Spurge

Maltese:
Tengħud tax-Xagħri

Scientific Name:
Euphorbia melitensis

Flowering period:
March to April

Status:
Frequent

Biotope:
Garrigue

Notes:
An endemic species. Usually the dominant species where it occurs

025 FG Flower close-up

026 FG A familiar sight along watercourses

026 FG Well established Reed beds are usually impenetrable

026 FG

English:
Great Reed

Maltese:
Qasba Kbira

Scientific Name:
Arundo donax

Flowering period:
September to October

Status:
Common

Biotope:
Along watercourses and in damp valleys

Notes:
Up to 400 cm high. Probably introduced. Used extensively in the making of windbreaks and the manufacture of blinds and artifacts

027 FG

English:
Pine Spurge

Maltese:
Tengħud Komuni

Scientific Name:
Euphorbia pinea

Flowering period:
All year round

Status:
Very common

Biotope:
Garrigue, steppe, but also in disturbed ground

Notes:
Base of stems and bottom leaves usually reddish

027 FG Pine Spurge prior to flowering

027 FG In flower

027 FG New growth

028 FG The Prickly Saltwort growing in a sand dune

028 FG

English:
Prickly Saltwort

Maltese:
Ħaxixa ta' l-Irmied
Xewwikija

Scientific Name:
Salsola kali

Flowering period:
May to October

Status:
Common

Biotope:
Sandy beaches

Notes:
An erect plant with a multi branched stem, found in most bays

029 FG Sizeable clump of the endangered Sea Spurge

029 FG Flower close up

029 FG New growth

029 FG

English:
Sea Spurge

Maltese:
Tengħud tar-Ramel

Scientific Name:
Euphorbia paralias

Flowering period:
April to September

Status:
Rare

Biotope:
Sand dunes

Notes:
Has become confined to one locality, and is considered as endangered

030 FG The Tree Spurge is the dominant species in certain localities

030 FG The flowers in spring

030 FG The fruit is to be found in late spring to early summer

030 FG

English:
Tree Spurge

Maltese:
Tengħud tas-Siġra

Scientific Name:
Euphorbia dendroides

Flowering period:
December to May

Status:
Frequent

Biotope:
Garrigue and valley walls

Notes:
Up to 200 cm high, forming a hemispherical shrub

030 FG In late summer the leaves start to sprout

031 FG Leaves of Black Bryony

031 FG Developing berries

031 FG Ripe Berries

031 FG

English:
Black Bryony

Maltese:
Brijonja Sewda

Scientific Name:
Tamus communis

Flowering period:
April to May

Status:
Rare

Biotope:
Maquis and valleys

Notes:
Produces small greenish flowers, followed by berries. Stem can be 400 cm long, usually climbing rocks or other plants

032 FG

English:
Sand Couch

Maltese:
Sikrana tar-Ramel

Scientific Name:
Elytrigia juncea

Flowering period:
April and June

Status:
Scarce and localised

Biotope:
Sand dunes

Notes:
Erect stems up to 80 cm long. Used to be much more common, but is now confined to only three localities

032 FG Typical stand of the Sand Couch

032 FG Close-up

Thistles

001 FT Spiny flower-head

001 FT

English:
Southern Star Thistle

Maltese:
Xewk ta' l-Għatba

Scientific Name:
Centaurea nicaeensis

Flowering period:
April to July

Status:
Common

Biotope:
Steppes, garrigue and abandoned agricultural land

Notes:
With branched stems up to 60 cm high. Sometimes grows close to the ground. A Mediterranean species

001 FT Sometimes grows low amongst vegetation

002 FT The spiny leaves of the Wild Artichoke

002 FT Early stages of flower-head development

002 FT Wild Artichoke flower-head developing

002 FT

English:
Wild Artichoke

Maltese:
Qaqoċċ tax-Xewk

Scientific Name:
Cynara cardunculus

Flowering period:
March to June

Status:
Common

Biotope:
Steppe, garrigue and clayey slopes

Notes:
A spectacular species, sometimes 100 cm high with large numbers of flower-heads. The leaves are also very spiny

002 FT The large flower of the Wild Artichoke

002 FT A Crown of thorns

002 FT The flower-heads attract large numbers of insects, especially beetles

002 FT By early summer the flower-head of the Wild Artichoke would have dried up

003 FT Boar Thistle flower

003 FT Leaf of the Boar Thistle

003 FT

English:
Boar Thistle

Maltese:
Xewk Abjad

Scientific Name:
Galactites tomentosa

Flowering period:
March to June, sometimes earlier

Status:
Very common

Biotope:
Grows everywhere, preferring disturbed ground

Notes:
Stems up to 65 cm high. The commonest species of thistle on the Islands. Found throughout the Mediterranean region

004 FT

English:
Horse Thistle

Maltese:
Xewk tax-Xitan

Scientific Name:
Notobasis syriaca

Flowering period:
January to May

Status:
Frequent

Biotope:
Damp valleys, country paths and roadsides

Notes:
Branched stems up to 180 cm high

004 FT Flower close-up

004 FT The leaves growing below the flower-heads are usually a pinkish violet

005 FT The broad, white veined and spiny leaves of the Milk Thistle

005 FT

English:
Milk Thistle

Maltese:
Xewk tal-Madonna

Scientific Name:
Silybum marianum

Flowering period:
April to June

Status:
Common

Biotope:
Disturbed ground and roadsides

Notes:
Up to 200 cm high. Large white veined leaves characteristic of species

005 FT Flower-head of the Milk Thistle

006 FT In its typical environment – sandy substrate

006 FT

English:
Sea Holly

Maltese:
Xewk ir-Ramel

Scientific Name:
Eryngium maritimum

Flowering period:
June to October

Status:
Rare

Biotope:
Sand dunes

Notes:
Up to 60 cm high. Due to its specialised Biotope the species is vulnerable and considered as endangered

006 FT The leaves are thick, rigid, sinuated and spiny

006 FT Sometimes the foliage of the Sea Holly has a bluish/purplish tinge

006 FT Close-up of small bluish flowers surrounded by purplish spiny bracts

007 FT Clustered Carline Thistle

007 FT Developing flower-head

007 FT Flower-head in full bloom

007 FT

English:
Clustered Carline Thistle

Maltese:
Sajtun

Scientific Name:
Carlina involucrata

Flowering period:
May to August

Status:
Common

Biotope:
Rocky valleys, steppes and long-abandoned fields

Notes:
Various stems arising out of underground rhizome. Can reach 80 cm in height. A species of the Mediterranean region

008 FT The Wooly Safflower growing in clumps

008 FT Flower close-up

008 FT

English:
Woolly Safflower

Maltese:
Xewk ta' Kristu

Scientific Name:
Carthamus lanatus ssp.baeticus

Flowering period:
May to July

Status:
Common

Biotope:
Steppes, clay slopes, abandoned fields and country paths

Notes:
Can be present in large numbers. Erect stem up to 60 cm high

009 FT Leaves of the Sand Oyster Thistle

009 FT Typical habitat of the species

009 FT Each plant can support large numbers of flowers

009 FT

English:
Sand Oyster Thistle

Maltese:
Xewk Isfar tar-Ramel

Scientific Name:
Scolymus hispanicus

Flowering period:
April to July

Status:
Scarce

Biotope:
Mostly sand dunes

Notes:
Another species that is vulnerable due to its specialised environment; currently very limited and rare, mostly due to human encroachment and interference

009 FT Flower of the Sand Oyster Thistle

010 FT

English:
Spotted Golden-thistle

Maltese:
Xewk Isfar

Scientific Name:
Scolymus maculatus

Flowering period:
April to July

Status:
Frequent

Biotope:
Valleys, clay slopes

Notes:
Can reach 90 cm in height. A species of the Mediterranean region

010 FT Winged stem, a characteristic of the species

010 FT Spotted Golden-thistle flower profile

010 FT Spotted Golden-thistle flower profile

010 FT Flower detail

011 FT

English:
Ground Thistle

Maltese:
Xewk tal-Miskta

Scientific Name:
Atractylis gummifera

Flowering period:
August to November

Status:
Common

Biotope:
Steppes and garrigue

Notes:
Ground hugging flower-heads bloom after all the leaves have dried up. The root is said to be poisonous

011 FT The flowers can be pink to purple as in this example

011 FT The Ground Thistle is usually found growing in groups

012 FT Showing the oblong heavily undulated and spiny leaves

012 FT

English:
Woolly Carline Thistle

Maltese:
Sebqet 'l Ommha

Scientific Name:
Carlina lanata

Flowering period:
May to July

Status:
Frequent

Biotope:
Abandoned fields, disturbed ground

Notes:
Up to 45 cm high. A Mediterranean species

012 FT Main stem can be up to 45 cm high

012 FT Florets are a purplish pink

012 FT Flower detail of the Woolly Carline Thistle

013 FT

English:
Slender Thistle

Maltese:
Xewk tal-Fjura żgħira

Scientific Name:
Carduus pycnocephalus

Flowering period:
March to June

Status:
Common

Biotope:
Roadsides and disturbed ground

Notes:
Winged stem up to 80 cm high

013 FT Flower-head close-up

013 FT Showing the spiny leaves of the Slender Thistle

Shrubs and Trees

001 FST Leaves and cones of the Aleppo Pine

001 FST

English:
Aleppo Pine

Maltese:
Siġra taż-Żnuber

Scientific Name:
Pinus halepensis

Flowering period:
Cones all year round

Status:
Common

Biotope:
Mostly forestation sites and large gardens

Notes:
Extinct in the wild but widely re-introduced. Evergreen tree, with male and female cones produced on the same tree

001 FST Dried cones

002 FST

English:
Sandarac

Maltese:
Siġra ta' l-Għargħar

Scientific Name:
Tetraclinis articulata

Flowering period:
November to December

Status:
Very rare

Biotope:
In the wild state grows in maquis

Notes:
The national tree. Evergreen, this tree rarely exceeds 10 metres in height. What was once a common tree is now reduced to a handful of small populations. Found only in Algeria, Morocco and in Europe, Malta and south east Spain

002 FST The Sandarac is protected by law

002 FST Female cones are up to 15 mm across, male cones 3mm

003 FST The Holly like leaves of the Evergreen Oak

003 FST

English:
Evergreen Oak

Maltese:
Siġra tal-Ballut

Scientific Name:
Quercus ilex

Flowering period:
Spring

Status:
Rare as a wild tree

Biotope:
Woodland

Notes:
Evergreen, growing considerably. A few remaining wild trees are hundreds of years old. Also known as the Holly Oak tree, because of the serrated and holly-like leaves, which are very variable. A Mediterranean species

004 FST Almond Tree flower buds

004 FST The hard hairy fruit with the edible kernel

004 FST Each tree bears hundreds of flowers

004 FST

English:
Almond Tree

Maltese:
Lewż

Scientific Name:
Prunus dulcis

Flowering period:
Winter

Status:
Common

Biotope:
Valleys, but also cultivated land

Notes:
Probably introduced, but naturalized all over the Islands. The tree is spectacular when in flower

005 FST

English:
Fig Tree

Maltese:
Siġra tat-Tin

Scientific Name:
Ficus carica

Flowering period:
Spring, flowers not visible, being enclosed in the fruit

Status:
Common

Biotope:
Valleys. maquis, cliff faces and disturbed ground

Notes:
A deciduous tree. Probably introduced, with different cultivars producing fruit that vary in colour, size and taste

005 FST The palmate leaves of the Fig tree

005 FST The fruit

006 FST Early stage of berries

006 FST

English:
Lentisk

Maltese:
Deru

Scientific Name:
Pistacia lentiscus

Flowering period:
January to April

Status:
Common

Biotope:
Maquis and rocky sides of valleys

Notes:
A small evergreen tree or shrub. Red berries form following pollination

006 FST Ripe berries

007 FST

English:
Hawthorn

Maltese:
Żagħrun

Scientific Name:
Crataegus monogyna

Flowering period:
March to May

Status:
Frequent

Biotope:
Valleys and maquis

Notes:
A small deciduous tree with 2 cm spines on the branches. The fruit ripens in autumn, turning red. The leaves are lobed. Also found in most of Europe and the Mediterranean region

007 FST Flowers of the Hawthorn

007 FST Leaves and fruit

008 FST The bark is smooth and silvery grey in colour

008 FST Naturalised Blue-leaved Acacia trees

008 FST

English:
Blue-leaved Acacia

Maltese:
Gazzija

Scientific Name:
Acacia cyanophylla

Flowering period:
March to April

Status:
Common

Biotope:
Widely planted, but also naturalized in valleys

Notes:
Fast growing tree, reaching 10 meters in height. Originally an Australian species

008 FST Flower detail

009 FST

English:
Pomegranate

Maltese:
Rummien

Scientific Name:
Punica granatum

Flowering period:
May to July

Status:
Common

Biotope:
As a wild shrub or tree found mostly in valleys and rocky slopes

Notes:
A deciduous tree or shrub. Widely naturalized. Cultivated for the fruit. Originally an Asian species

009 FST Pomegranate flowers are up to 4 cm across

009 FST The sweet pulp surrounding the seeds is a reddish purple

010 FST

English:
Bay Laurel

Maltese:
Siġra tar-Rand

Scientific Name:
Laurus nobilis

Flowering period:
February to April

Status:
Scarce as a wild tree

Biotope:
Valleys and maquis, also in large gardens

Notes:
A native species. Evergreen tree, up to 20 meters high. The leaves are dark green with wavy edges and very aromatic, traditionally used in stews. Fruit 15 mm, black when ripe

010 FST The fruit turns black when ripe

010 FST New leaves are red

010 FST Bay Laurel leaves have wavy edges

011 FST

English:
Mediterranean Buckthorn

Maltese:
Alaternu

Scientific Name:
Rhamnus alaternus

Flowering period:
January to March

Status:
Scarce

Biotope:
Valley beds and maquis

Notes:
Evergreen shrub up to 500 cm high. Flowers develop into purplish red, eventually black berry like fruit. This and the other Rhamnus species is the larval food plant of the Cleopatra Butterfly, **Gonepteryx cleopatra**

011 FST The berry like fruit

012 FST Tender new Carob leaves

012 FST Pods or Locust Beans used to be an important ingredient in the fodder fed to cows and other farm animals

012 FST

English:
Carob

Maltese:
Siġra tal-Ħarrub

Scientific Name:
Ceratonia siliqua

Flowering period:
October to November. Male and female flowers appear on different trees, the well known pods forming on female trees

Status:
Common

Biotope:
Valleys, maquis, cultivated land

Notes:
This is in fact also an introduced species, but to-day it is hard to imagine our countryside without this tree. It is very sad to see many of these trees uprooted and destroyed in the name of progress

013 FST

English:
White Poplar

Maltese:
Siġra tal-Luq

Scientific Name:
Populus alba

Flowering period:
Early spring

Status:
This species is rare in the wild state

Biotope:
When wild it grows along watercourses

Notes:
Deciduous. The leaves are dark green above and silvery white on the underside, due to a dense covering of short hairs. Another characteristic of the species is the smooth, light grey bark

013 FST White Poplar leaves are a dark green from above

013 FST And white on the underside

014 FST

English:
Olive-leaved Buckthorn

Maltese:
Żiju

Scientific Name:
Rhamnus oleoides

Flowering period:
February to April

Status:
Frequent

Biotope:
Maquis and garrigue

Notes:
Low lying shrub, usually not higher than 100 cm. A characteristic of this species are the numerous hard branches that are spiny at the tips. The leaves are small. A Mediterranean species

014 FST The branches of the Olive-leaved Buckthorn are spiny

015 FST Normal yellow flower

015 FST The scarcer reddish flower

015 FST

English:
Prickly Pear

Maltese:
Bajtar tax-Xewk

Scientific Name:
Opuntia ficus-indica

Flowering period:
May to July

Status:
Common

Biotope:
Along field edges and rubble walls

Notes:
Frequently cultivated for the fruit and as a windbreak but also widely naturalised. A native of Tropical America

015 FST Sometimes forms a large bush. The large pads are stems, and the spines are reduced leaves

016 FST

English:
Olive Tree

Maltese:
Siġra taż-Żebbuġ

Scientific Name:
Olea europaea

Flowering period:
March to May

Status:
Scarce as a wild tree

Biotope:
Maquis, woodland, and also cultivated

Notes:
Evergreen. Known to live for hundreds of years. The cultivation and oil production was of big economic importance in Malta and Gozo, as evidenced by the names of villages such as Żebbuġ (Olive) in Malta, Żebbuġ (Olive) in Gozo, and Żejtun (Żejt meaning Oil)

016 FST The fruit, cultivated all across the Mediterranean

017 FST

English:
African Tamarisk

Maltese:
Siġra tal-Bruk

Scientific Name:
Tamarix africana

Flowering period:
February to June

Status:
Wild trees are rare, but large numbers have been planted in forestation projects

Biotope:
Coastal, especially in salt marshes and sand dunes

Notes:
The numerous branches are covered with small leaves. Flowers can be white or pink. Can tolerate very saline conditions, including sea spray. Of interest as well is the amount of dew that the leaves can hold even late into the morning, providing water for fauna in otherwise dry conditions

017 FST Tamarisk growing in typical habitat

017 FST Flowers can be white or pink

018 FST Leaves of Bramble

018 FST Stem with thorns

018 FST Bramble flower

018 FST Bramble flower

018 FST

English:
Bramble

Maltese:
Għolliq

Scientific Name:
Rubus ulmifolius

Flowering period:
April to October

Status:
Common

Biotope:
Maquis and valley beds

Notes:
A climber, with the dense thorny stems creating natural barriers in some valleys. The fruit is edible

018 FST The edible fruit

019 FST Wolfbane fruit resembles a pair of horns

019 FST Wolfbane flowers and seed on the same plant

019 FST The seeds with silky hairs to aid dispersal

019 FST

English:
Wolfbane

Maltese:
Siġra tal-Ħarir

Scientific Name:
Periploca angustifolia

Flowering period:
Autumn to Spring

Status:
Frequent

Biotope:
Maquis, garrigue

Notes:
A large dense shrub, sometimes up to 200 cm high. Horn like seed pods split to release hundreds of seeds with white silky hairs to facilitate wind dispersal

019 FST A species of Bug **Caenocoris nerii** has built a relationship with the Wolfbane, having the nymph mimic the seeds in colour, shape and size, presumably to escape predators

020 FST The ovate leaves can be 10 cm long

020 FST Fruit close-up

020 FST

English:
Quince

Maltese:
Sfarġel

Scientific Name:
Cydonia oblonga

Flowering period:
March to May

Status:
Scarce

Biotope:
Naturalised in some valleys

Notes:
A native of Central Asia but cultivated in many parts of the world. Tree up to 600 cm high. Fruit is covered with a dense matted hairiness. The Quince is used as wild stock for grafting Apple, Pear and other fruit trees

021 FST Photo shows leaves borne in opposite pairs

021 FST

English:
Evergreen Honeysuckle

Maltese:
Qarn il-Mogħża

Scientific Name:
Lonicera implexa

Flowering period:
April to May

Status:
Frequent

Biotope:
Maquis, garrigue, valley sides

Notes:
Large evergreen shrub. In certain localities it is the dominant shrub

021 FST Detail of the flower of the Evergreen Honeysuckle

021 FST Maltese name refers to the shape of the buds

022 FST

English:
Rosemary

Maltese:
Klin

Scientific Name:
Rosmarinus officinalis

Flowering period:
All year round

Status:
Scarce

Biotope:
Maquis

Notes:
Forms a dense strongly aromatic shrub up to 200 cm high. Leaves used as herb. A species of the Mediterranean region

022 FST The leaves of the Rosemary are strongly aromatic

023 FST Forms dense impenetrable shrubs

023 FST

English:
Shrubby Orache

Maltese:
Bjanka

Scientific Name:
Atriplex halimus

Flowering period:
August to November

Status:
Common

Biotope:
Coastal, from clay slopes to sand and rocky areas

Notes:
Forms dense shrubs 250 cm high in places. Used to be rarer, but now widely planted

023 FST Leaf close-up

024 FST

English:
Maltese Salt-tree

Maltese:
Xebb

Scientific Name:
Darniella melitensis

Flowering period:
July to October

Status:
Locally common

Biotope:
Coastal cliffs

Notes:
Endemic. Described as recently as 1976. Grows into a dense shrub up to 250 cm high. Flowers small. Fruits in autumn

024 FST Shrub in typical habitat

024 FST Close-up of small fleshy leaves

025 FST Leaves of Grape Vine

025 FST

English:
Grape Vine

Maltese:
Dielja

Scientific Name:
Vitis vinifera

Flowering period:
April to May

Status:
Frequent as naturalised

Biotope:
Valleys, maquis and field margins

Notes:
Widely cultivated in many varieties, but has become naturalized

025 FST Fruit

026 FST The large palmate leaves

026 FST

English:
Castor Oil Tree

Maltese:
Siġra tar-Riċnu

Scientific Name:
Ricinus communis

Flowering period:
February to October

Status:
Common

Biotope:
Damp valley bottoms and disturbed ground

Notes:
Shrub up to 400 cm high. Large leaves palmate. The fruit is spiny. The seed is poisonous. An introduced species

Lower Plants

001 FLP

English:
Ink-cap

Maltese:
Faqqieh tal-Inka

Scientific Name:
Coprinus micaceus

Status:
Scarce

Biotope:
Valleys and gardens

Notes:
Large numbers of this species can appear when conditions are right, usually the dense clusters found growing beneath trees or on rotting trunks

001 FLP The Ink-cap usually grows in dense clusters

002 FLP

English:
Sand Mushroom

Maltese:
—

Scientific Name:
Montagnites arenaria

Status:
Very rare

Biotope:
Sand dunes

Notes:
Gives the impression of being shrivelled. Very rare due to its specialised habitat requirements

002 FLP Looking wilted and shrivelled

002 FLP A mushroom with specific habitat requirements

003 FLP Showing the gills of this species

003 FLP

English:
Oyster Mushroom

Maltese:
Faqqiegħ tal-Ferla

Scientific Name:
Pleurotus eryngii ssp. ferulae

Status:
Scarce

Biotope:
Garrigue, maquis and fallow fields

Notes:
One of the larger mushrooms, with caps exceeding 15 cm. Grows low, with a short stalk. Grows and extracts nutrients from the roots of the Giant Fennel. Very variable in shape and size

003 FLP Thick leathery appearance of the ground hugging caps

004 FLP

English:
—

Maltese:
—

Scientific Name:
Inocype sp

Status:
Frequent

Biotope:
Wooded areas especially along footpaths

Notes:
Poisonous

004 FLP Some mushrooms can only be identified to species level by dissection. This Inocype sp. is one of them

004 FLP These mushrooms should not be eaten as they are poisonous

005 FLP Close-up

005 FLP

English:
Bracket Fungus

Maltese:
Lixka

Scientific Name:
Ganoderma sp

Status:
Scarce

Biotope:
Wooded areas and old mature gardens

Notes:
Grows on trunks of living trees, from where it gets the necessary nutrients, forming a number of shelves in large specimens

005 FLP Large specimen here growing on Tree trunk

006 FLP The Rose-gilled Grisette has the traditional mushroom shape

006 FLP Close-up of gills

006 FLP

English:
Rose-gilled Grisette

Maltese:
Faqqieħ tal-Ġonna

Scientific Name:
Volvariela speciosa

Status:
Frequent

Biotope:
Fields, gardens and other disturbed ground

Notes:
Another large species, with the cap, borne on a long stalk reaching 15 cm

007 FLP

English:
Cramp Balls

Maltese:
Ballun tas-Siġar

Scientific Name:
Daldinia concentrica

Status:
Rare

Biotope:
Lives on trunks and branches of dead trees

Notes:
Resembles a tar ball, sometimes having a diameter of 6 to 8 cm

007 FLP A number of Cramp Balls growing on a dead trunk

008 FLP Orange coloured – usually grows on rocks and stones

008 FLP

English:
Wall Xanthoria

Maltese:
Ksantorja

Scientific Name:
Xanthoria sp

Status:
Common

Biotope:
On rocks and tree-trunks

Notes:
Various similar species which are difficult to identify. The Xanthorias can be peeled off from the surface they are growing on. Colour can be orange or greenish

008 FLP Green coloured – usually grows on tree trunks

009 FLP

English:
—

Maltese:
—

Scientific Name:
Caloplaca sp

Status:
Common

Biotope:
On rocks

Notes:
Unlike the Xanthoria, these lichens which are similar are very flat and difficult to peel off. They sometimes make interesting patterns

009 FLP Different tones of orange to yellows

009 FLP A near perfect circle formed by this Lichen

010 FLP The photo shows three different species of fungi and lichens on the same branch: a Cramp Ball, Xanthoria and Ramalina

010 FLP

English:
Ramalina

Maltese:
Ramalina

Scientific Name:
Ramalina durieui

Status:
Scarce

Biotope:
Valleys and wooded areas, only on branches of trees

Notes:
Not found in many places, very distinctive

References

Baldacchino, A.E., Lanfranco, E. & Schembri, P.J. 1990. **Appuntamenti man-Natura**. Malta: Merlin Library.

Baldacchino, A.E. & Stevens, D.T. 2000. **Is-Siġar Maltin – l-użu u l-importanza**. Malta: Dipartiment għall-Ħarsien ta' l-Ambjent.

Cassar, L.F. & Stevens, D.T. 2002. **Coastal sand dunes under siege: a guide to conservation for environmental managers**. Malta. International Environment Institute, Foundation for International Studies.

Haslam, S.M., Sell, P.D. & Wolseley, P.A. 1977. **A Flora of the Maltese Islands**. Malta: Malta University Press.

Lanfranco, E. & Lanfranco, G. 2003. **Il-Flora Maltija.** Malta. Pubblikazzjonijiet Indipendenza (Kullana Kulturali No. 47).

Lanfranco, G. 1993. **Ħxejjex Mediċinali u Oħrajn fil-Gżejjer Maltin**. Malta: Media Centre Publications.

Lanfranco, G.G. 1969. **Field guide to the Wild Flowers of Malta**. Malta: Progress Press.

Lanfranco, S. 2002. **L-Ambjent Natural tal-Gżejjer Maltin**. Malta. Pubblikazzjonijiet Indipendenza (Kullana Kulturali No. 45).

Mifsud, M. 1999. **Closeups of Maltese Flora and Fauna**. Malta: Media Centre Publications.

Schembri, P.J. & Baldacchino, A.E. 1992. **Ilma, Blat u Ħajja**. Malta. Malta University Services Ltd.

Schembri, P.J. & Sultana, J. (eds.) 1989. **Red Data Book for the Maltese Islands**. Malta: Department of Information.

Sultana, J (ed) 1995. **Flora u Fawna ta' Malta**. Malta. Dipartiment għall-Ħarsien ta' l-Ambjent.

Sultana, J. & Falzon, V. (eds.) 2002. **Wildlife of the Maltese Islands**. Malta. Birdlife Malta,

Nature Trust, Malta.

Index of English Names

Index of Maltese Names

Index of Scientific Names